Not From Where I Sit

SAM CHRISTIAN IN, 'HIS OWN WORDS'

BARRY D. WADE

outskirtspress
DENVER, COLORADO

Outskirts Press, Inc.
http://www.outskirtspress.com

Paperback ISBN: 978-1-4787-6819-7
Hardback ISBN: 978-1-4787-6931-6

Outskirts Press and the "OP" logo are trademarks belonging to Outskirts Press, Inc.

PRINTED IN THE UNITED STATES OF AMERICA

'Look at me, you know what you see.', James Brown, 'The Boss'

'Not from where, I sit.' in his own, words', Sam Christian

I t was his eyes. I had seen them twenty-two years prior when, I had glanced upon them for the first time. They bore a look of alertness. A ubiquitously and small thing, if you should have just been seeing in the vain, physical and crass sense of the term.

Rather, it was an alertness on a much more deeper and profound spiritual sense.

Now, as I did then, what I saw in them, troubled my heart and made me feel ashamed of my own self. I saw that I, like so many others, had instantaneously hurt and offended him. And again, with that also, it was not as in the same ubiquitously vain and crass physical sense of the term either. Because in them again, like so many others, I had also found cordiality as well as that receptiveness.

And yet once again; like so many others, I, like a child in trance of something awe-inspiring or gawker at the scene of a vehicle accident, let myself or chose instead, got swept into the awe and reverence of the power inclusive to the 'things,' and legends associated with him.

Such an eclipse was this reverence and awe that I again like so many others, had selfishly or carelessly failed or neglected to take into consideration that despite all of those things associated with and because of this man, before us has, and still stands a man, nothing more or nothing less.

This leads to a mildly sad look in those eyes that I glance upon now as, I had back those twenty- two years prior. It appears to be a look of mild yet, patient dismay. Having had this second opportunity to meet and a more profound one to sit down with this man, I feel somewhat confident if not all-together comfortable now, in stating that this look has been oft-times and many of them in error, characterized as arrogance and indifference. Make no mistake about it, there is exceedingly immense power associated with this man. Unlike a lot of others though, after having had this second opportunity to sit down with this man, I have come to learn that that too, in addition to that likened to was beyond that of the vain, crass, physical sense as well.

Notwithstanding, I see in them as well, beyond that of the vain and physical sense also, a great number of other things. To name a few, I see in them life, respect, respect for life, loyalty, humility, determination as well as, a number of other things that one may perchance find in other people's eyes. I see in them also, conviction. In that regard again, though not in the vain, crass or otherwise ubiquitously physical sense of the term.

Having again, this second opportunity to sit with this man, and observe or purview the conviction or constitution in those eyes, this and those other characteristics as well, as the other things rumored, alleged or made-up compels me to do one other thing out of a sense of responsibility. Having had been bestowed with this now opportunity of interview, it compels me to look inward, or to pose those questions in regard to these characteristics to my own self in as well, as to you, the reader. It further, causes me to address my own sincerity or convictions in standing up for, or by them. It was at that point, before we had even started the interview that I had one, realized the gravity and responsibility of the golden opportunity that I had been given.

Then two, I then, realized that I had been blessed almost beyond all the vain, crass and worldly things in this world save one. That one thing is, the abridgement between here, in the existential sense of the term and the 'here-after' one. That one thing was, the power of information.

Finally, and thirdly, there was one other thing that I had realized upon that second meeting or chance of interview with this powerful man. And that was, that I had to allay all the crass and vain feelings of awe and reverence, if I were to do this man, myself and any who mayhap read this a service in sharing this information in a concise and correct manner to the best of my ability.

Of those three realizations, the most difficult to realize would have been the latter, had it not been for this man himself and another innate and almost eminent thing that I also saw in those powerful eyes. An unimaginable thing it was too, if one were to, just fall prey to, or accept the popular sentiment in regard to this man. In addition to the above and beyond all those other characteristics in the most humane, humble and spiritual sense there was also, love in those eyes.

How he would assist me in seeing in this regard, is one of the most profound, strange and funny things that I have ever seen. Psychology has it that, when a person averts eye to eye contact or their eyes wonder towards a certain direction when they are speaking to someone that they are in some way telling an un-truth or lie. There is one jocular note that I would like to offer up on this before expounding further on this serious and important tome. 'What of psychology then, when a person is blind'?

When it came to Suleiman or Sam, as he is more familiarly and widely known, I had found a wide contradiction to that assertion. As I had come to learn upon my interview with him, Sam does this as a way to make the party that he is speaking to, feel at ease without that sense of awe associated with at being in his presence. This desire or chore, is not something that is exclusively held by Sam as, many can attest to, when they are cast into the public spotlight whether in the cast of renowned, famed or infamy. Like those others, by doing this, he and the party conversing can have a clear and coherent dialogue. It's been said that, 'You can't know an individual until you know where they have come from, or what they have been through.' This man, knows exactly who he is, and what he has been through. He is also aware and cognizant too, of what we, the public have portrayed, alleged or rumored him to be as well. He has long ago, made peace with that and himself as he knows that, regardless of whatever has transpired for him in this world, ultimately and with surety, the most ultimate judgment lies well beyond whatever judgment that you or I could ever place upon him on or in this plane called, life. He has come to know and learn also that, as he has relayed to me, "By virtue of all of those things melded together and having had survived them, that it was, and had become an inevitable responsibility and duty to share my experience in its proper perspective of example of not so much as to, 'how' or, 'how not to', but rather, in conviction and cause and one's desire, will and determination to stand firm upon them. If, in the midst of that, one should find example of 'whether to' or 'whether not to' then, all the more for the blessings." Paramount above that though, he wants it noted and relayed that, no matter what the cause, reason or desire, make it for a positive, righteous or just one. All my life, I had longed for just such an opportunity. We had both found it funny and humbling that, he had also. For me, it was, in wanting to tell a great and profound story and for him it was, in wanting it told correctly. And although not verbalized between the two of us, we had both wanted it told beyond the ubiquitous, vain and crass physical sense of the term. So, it was with this opportunity and him being who he was, neither of us, was my fondest desire and wish would be denied at its conclusion.

Upon our meeting, and before we had begun interviewing, I had noted an eerily coincidental event and feeling of 'Deja-vu' in one of the first things that he had said to me. "It's not important whether you are a Christian, Jewish or a Muslim. What's important is that, you have a relationship with God." Seven hours prior in the wee hours before even the Fajar prayer, my mother, a pianist in church for a long number of years until recently, had said the exact same thing to me. Up until that point to my knowledge, neither of them had ever met face to face before. And so, we began.

"Brother Beyah, a lot of the youth and especially the young men in this world these days have got the game twisted up would you agree? And if so, could you give us your take on this perception?"

Humbly, and looking an aged version of the man of strength and power that he has been rumored, alleged and legend to be given, the things circulated about him and seemingly, with the patience of 'Job' he begins with his ritual to make one feel at ease.

Softly, he averts his gaze downward and with equally soft verbalization of concurrence and agreement he responds, "That's right, sure." "My first question Brother Beyah is, how was it for you, and what was Philadelphia like when you were growing up? My second part of that question Sir is, how did it feel growing up in the Philadelphia that you grew up in?" With his response, he starts off as he would in practically all of his responses with, a kind word. "It's been a blessing" he responds as his gaze slowly and kindly rises back up to meet mine's before kindly and softly returning back earthward.

"And, a lesson!" he adds, with surety of emphasis and conviction as his gaze then bounces upward beating to meet mine's. This action in conjunction with the person from whom it is coming from, then seems to serve as a very discernible and emphatic exclamation on a very profound and important point. His gaze then, no longer looked downward or, towards me, but as if long and way back into a or, more poignantly, his Past. After that millisecond of self-reflection he then added, "As you know or may have heard, I found out the hard way." As I, from the stories, rumors and the likes, had to surely concur with, I then posed my query for which, I had based my own desires and longings for this, and just such a meeting. I first responded, "And, as you may, or may not know, that by doing so, you have led a comparably equal number of young men to good works as well as, those that you are said to have led astray or to the nefarious?" For this, again, he defers the credit, "Praise be to God!" At first, I found it particularly odd that, he specifically stated, 'God' not, Allah when he said, 'Praise be to God!'. I emphasize this point because of him being a Muslim, and as being such, they, as you may or may not know, refer to, or use the term or title, Allah when referring to the Creator or God. As I later found, he would alternate between the usage of the term, Allah or, God as a form of declaration while keeping mindful, of the one-ness or singular of the deity's might. Apples and oranges. You say Tomato, I say 'Toemahto' as long, as we each, reach the same destination or common ground.

Expounding on growing up in the Philadelphia that he grew up in, he then goes on to lament that, "They had nothing but gangs! Gangs on every corner!" When he spoke of the different gangs I was then compelled, to wonder or ponder aloud considering, Philadelphia being a fabric of different cultures especially, in South Philadelphia about the interaction of races in regard to the gangs. This, he deftly pounces upon to clear up any misconceptions that anything that he did was motivated or based on the race of another people. "No, there were no racial lines, there were just gangs on every block or 'corner'." While he is relaying this, he is gesturing with his hands to, exemplify the divisions or dissections of the blocks or corners. As I am listening and watching intently, my mind goes back to him telling me of his first meeting with his life-long friend and brother, Donnie Day as his arms are moving rhythmically and geometrically in precision movements likened to, that of a boxer or pugilist. Born, Samuel Christian Jr. on March 20th, 1939, Sam or Beyah, was one of three children born under the union of his father and mother, Samuel Christian Sr. and Helen Christian. Raised with his two sisters, Coretta and Sandra, Sam, with a wide beaming smile and eyes to match then, happily and almost excitedly exclaims to me, "My two sisters were my two best friends!" Then broadening his smile, he goes on to add, "It was because of them that, I was never without a girlfriend!" However, Sam's love for his sisters and theirs for him goes much metaphysically deeper than that. He then goes on to, relay to me the story of how, when he was younger and getting chastised with a belt by his father, that they would cry.

As he relayed it to me, "they would actually be crying and screaming as if it were they, who were getting hit." He then, shakes his head before me, in sincere and sheer befuddlement as he goes on to lament,

"That's one of the things that I've never understood." This makes me smile, as he goes on further to relay, and with his eternal self-query, " I used to ask them, 'I'm getting the whooping, why are you all crying?'" Still relaying and wondering aloud he goes on and states, "I used to ask them, 'what, are you all feeling the hits on your bodies too?'" None of them, through their lives, has ever been fully able to explain this phenomenon to the other.

For the record, what made this thing so mind-boggling and perplexing to them was that, neither of Sam's sisters ever received physical punishment or chastisement from or, at the hands of their father or mother. Nor, did he witness it against his mother either. Sam was the only one that held that distinction or, was given that honor, in their household.

This was not to say however, that there were no mis-communications or mixed signals or what- have-you in their home. There was the one time when, a very young Sam, had witnessed his father after drinking, having cross-words with his mother. Sam probably, wouldn't have been able to have with-stood that beating being so young, and with his diminutive frame had his father decided to physically direct his anger then at him, ran to his mother's side and aid.

After leaving the house and returning, the first, and only person that Sam's father wanted to speak with was Sam. Sitting Sam upon his knee, his father then looked Sam squarely in the eyes and apologized to him for his display in the home. "I never forgot that." he tells me, looking me squarely in the eye with a look of proud gratitude and appreciation.

While relaying this, there is a look etched on his face as if, there were some message or lesson that I should have been deciphering from that recollection. As I was to find out from him very soon, and as I have learned throughout life that, there was.

Then there was another or, that other time, when he was a little bit older and once again, he thought his father was going to lay hands to his mother. This time however, there was no tender or poignant moment afterwards as Sam then, found a bed slat and actually did, make connection with it over his Father's head.

Connected to religion since birth (a connection he has not lost to this Day), Beyah or Sam, as young boy dutifully, right along with his sisters Coretta, Sandra and their mother attended church.

On Sunday mornings, they as well as others in their South Philly neighborhood, would congregate at Mount Olive Temple church there.

Although when we began and I not knowing, (because of that 'trance' or, 'gawker' Complex) how to proceed, I asked him a series of questions while searching for a place to delve. I remember now, as I have written about Sam, his mother's, his sibling's and his, connection to religion and his response to one of my queries that day.

"Your Physical self, has to stay connected to your spiritual self."

Expounding further, he then went on to state that, "its imperative, if you want to hold-fast to God." During our next meeting, we were discussing women and he stated, "Woman, is the connection to the Spirit. That is why, she must be put, first." Later during that conversation he goes on to state that, "When you see a woman, you should see your own mother."

Now although I am no renowned theologian or psychologist, I would venture at this point the risk to say that, this is my belief as to why and how, Sam has been gifted with and has kept that Innate connection to both. That innate inter-action of feelings for, and of the spiritual familial love and support did not just extend to the women in Sam's home either.

This, I will expound on in a bit. Before I leave this point for a bit though, I would like to bring to light a certain revelation that I was compelled to recall that was revealed to me long ago, and that I had forgotten about.

When I was younger, and would see the women that were the

mates of men in the Nation of Islam, I noticed two distinct things. First, they did not look 'beat-down' in any stretch of the word physically or imagination into submissiveness. In fact, to me, most bore the look of dignity and regality, (I imagine hence, the faddish hip-hop term, 'My Queen' before, that actual lexicon lost its meaning and luster.) Then there was second, I had not at that time, seen or heard of them being mentally or physically beaten on or upon. Now, this observation to me, remained true until I had spoken in depth about this observation to one of Sam's former wives.

Several people come in while we are talking today. To my knowledge while I was present, they had not been verbally, telephonically, electronically, written or even, 'smoke-signaled' summoned, but they were summoned today. I know this too, beyond the crass, vain and physical sense. I know this because, as we were discussing his religious and familial connections, and the imperativeness of staying connected a couple of days earlier, he had said something. "One of the things my mother always stressed was, 'Always take care of the poor, needy, orphan or the wayfarer.' "He then went on in stating, "She used to take care of orphans as well as, kids from the neighborhood." As if, already knowing and anticipating my surprise (no, 'Cry me a River' story here.), Sam was not in-opulent or destitute growing up. So, to lay in-opulence as one of the reason for, things turning out the way that they would, for Sam in the future, could not be used as a valid reason or excuse. Taking his cue from my raised eyebrow, he then goes on and states that, "There was this one girl that my mother used to take care of. She would be on post everyday waiting for me after school as she was instructed to by my mother." "You mean, you had to pick her up and walk her home from school?" "Yep, that's right! And she was always on post waiting for me too, right where she was supposed to be. Thelma, was her name. I haven't seen her, in a while. She was Always one of my strongest defenders. She used to say, 'I'm tired of people misusing my brother's name.'" When I walked in to see him on this particular day, excitedly he began, "Remember the girl, Thelma that I told you about? She called, and said she'd been trying to get in touch with me for a while. She's coming over today.

She said that she, had a gift for me." When Thelma came in that day, I quickly noted Sam's exponential and resultant effect of the spiritual, familial and of how, the woman plays and displays, a major part in the connection of the scheme of it all.

Upon her and I initially meeting, I felt eyes upon me seemingly akin to, those of a lioness surveying a dangerous predator or foe in the presence of one of her cubs. She then, cordially, but with no less leeriness and surveillance introduced herself. She warmed up considerably and became respectfully receptive after with his nod of concurrence, I explained what I had been endeavoring to do. I asked Thelma a number of the questions that I had and would be asking Sam as well, as the host of the others of whom, he would consider close in his intimate circle. The questions that I had formed, I felt, would give me insight into my main objective for presenting this prose of this man without the legend, fascination, or hoopla, that has been associated with him.

Furthermore, I had formed them to affirm or re-enforce the objective of my secondary reason for writing this prose. That was of, and in conviction or constitution and one's sincerity and willingness against all odds to stand firm upon, or strong in defense of either, and to pose the question to the reader, if faced with the same circumstances that he had been face with, or had went through, what if any, would be the outcome? The questions that I had formed, I also felt would give us the inquisitive, nosey, curious and oft-times, insensitive outside public an un- adulterated, personal view on Sam from his perspective in regard to his character, feelings and belief system without again, the legend, fascination, hoopla or conviction of us, the public concerned with, and in regard to, the things that went on went him.

And finally, of those in his intimate circle, again as a sample of you and I the curious public, I formed them also, as an indicator of my second reason for this endeavor as I thought to myself, 'where from a better place, than those there with him' could I get again, in an un-adulterated and poignant fashion, the most unadulterated, objective and impartial answer as an example of you and I, the general public in regard to the man behind the legend, fascination and hoopla.

As many of those intimates in some manner, form or fashion have moved on, or have transcended to other places, or things, I asked them of how, or what effect did the things that went on with Sam or that had happened with Sam's life play in their lives, or way of thinking.

The vectors, questions or points of reference that I had formulat-ed, were chosen, to gain and give insight into the totality of the man behind the myth or legends that were bore, or were the results of, or, from thoughts or things that I through my own personal life, have tried ascribed to as a view, of morality that may be evinced to show as a moral compass, the make up of, being.

These things, reasons or choices that I have chosen, I have done so in case, or, if one should decide to, for whatever the reason, judge my ultimate objective for having and making the most of this golden opportunity to delve into the psyche of, what is the make-up of what lies fundamentally in most of us, in regard to conviction.

Those vectors or points of reference that I had or were chosen, are or were as follows; Life, Respect, Loyalty, Family, Caring, Devotion, Gratitude, Humility, Determination, Conviction and, Love. In re-gard to Thelma, without first, having had the opportunity to have heard her response to any of these things, I was humbled and glad that my intentions were, and are righteous and just.

Before we get to that part in regard to the responses, if I may take the liberty, I want to go on first in giving a little more chronological history of the man behind the legend and myth. Sam's first job was with his uncle whom, was what we at that time, in our urban environ called, a 'Huckster'.

He had one of those old 'Man-powered' push-carts or wagons if you will. He used to sell fruits and vegetables. As he is telling me this, he is looking as if to ascertain, if the word or term, 'Huckster' would be alien to me or if, I were old enough to recall it. I smile deeply, with reminiscence and recollection as I recall, the many trips down to 9th & Washington Avenue with my own father and finish for him, "Huckster" This time it is he, who looks at me with a small amount of reverential pride at my remembrance. It was sort of like, the way a kindergarten teacher or, a pleasantly surprised parent may look upon a child, at having made an astute observation. Another funny thing happened at this point. Although, we were several feet apart and across a good sized table without the ability of physical reach or touch, he then hugged me. At this point, he may have as well, 'Walked on air'. It is here where, with my spiritual and physical eyes, I actually see, the 'Myth' dissipate from around him as, he steps forward and presents himself, his trust, assistance, his support and all the resources in his power or word to help bring to fruition this endeavor, that I had sought to embark upon.

In that instant as, and when he had done all that, he had not moved an inch.

Before my eyes, he had then granted to me in, not only the physical and ephemeral, but esoteric and spiritual life-long sense as well, this favor. It was then, that he and I, Samuel Beyah Christian and myself became eternally connected. As to the term 'Huckster', I remembered also fondly, and appreciatively that two dollars that, I would receive from Stanley or, 'How many' that used to traverse through my own hometown which, was not too far from Sam's own South Philadelphia neighborhood for working with him on those Saturday mornings, when I myself, was a kid.

Upon relaying his next statement to me, he looked at me with a look, I would come to know well over the course of my sitting down with him. He looked at me as if, it were a question or test for, and of the listener or, of one's ability or capability to grasp the understanding of the human nature or more profoundly, the finite and spiritual inter-workings of it.

He relayed to me that, "When we used to walk down the street, my uncle used to throw potatoes at the kids that used to run up to the cart." Being the person that I had first met, and making concession or granting solace and forgiveness for the acts or responses of human nature, he then added, "He did this because, and he didn't want the kids to come up and harass or bother me."

Now, where the look of 'lesson' came into play was, as he was stating this it read, 'for as fervent with gallant intentions that this act was', it fell short even to him then, in astuteness to throw one's lively-hood in goods away. We both laughed, although not audibly at the foolishness of this act as his expression read, 'If you're going to throw it away, you might as well give it away to possibly, receive, recompense, favor or reward in return for it'.

I cannot help but to think, that it was at this time where Sam, had developed one of those concepts or attributes also reputed or rumored, about him.

His second job was at a clothing factory located at 1309 Noble Street.

There, he was employed by a man named, Tom Levin. Between Tom, and some guys whose names he said were, the Cappicci brothers, Sam(Joe's Brother) and Joe whose business had merged together with Tom Levin's had procreated and generated a great number of lively-hoods throughout South Philly and surrounding parts of the city.

During the 'Black power' movement of the 60's, Tom Levin called Sam into his office, and with awareness of the profundity of how monumental that it, the movement and, or the over-all changes that block in time would bring, stated to Sam in the form of proclamation and promise, "Sam, I don't care what happens with what's going on out there and or, if I have to fire everyone else, you will always have a job here." This promise, and Sam being who he was, and probable or possibly having, a glimpse or glimmer of how monumentally defined he was destined to be knew, was sincere. Also during this movement and time, Sam had also made it a practice to periodically or, more like clockwork stop by the then called, 'Employment office' to check out or to ascertain the status of any jobs that may perchance benefit or assist some deserving or needy party or family in the neighborhood. As to Levin's promise, Sam also knew that, that too, would not come to pass either at that time. In 1963, after having never lost his thirst and desire of spiritual connection while seeking knowledge of self, Sam began researching and finally interacting with the Moor's Science Temple which, was located at 2012 South Street. He was introduced to the religion there by one, Kenyatta and Alma Bey. It was through Alma, Kenyatta's wife that, Sam would meet a number of the people that would also make vast impacts in his life.

These folks were, the 'tops' in their businesses and at who they were, or would become to Sam.

Although he did not expound or elaborate on it, no doubt presuming correctly that, if I did not know, I would research on it so that, I could relay to you in case, you may not have knowledge on or know who, the Moors were. I hurriedly brushed up again, on my knowledge by opening for starters, the dictionary.

The Moors were a Muslim people of the Northwest Africa region. As it had been chronicled, they fought against colonialism. Colonialism as defined in the dictionary was or is, 'a system by which, a country maintains foreign colonies especially, for economic exploitation'. The Moors were led by one, Jumbo Kenyatta. The name Jumbo Kenyatta means, 'Flaming Spear'. It was from Jumbo Kenyatta whom, Kenyatta Beyah adopted his name from. In 1965, with the knowledge he had gained from The Moors Science Temple, Sam then, with all the devotion and fervor that he had exhibited while attending there and church with his mother and sisters embraced the religion of Islam as he grasped and knew it to be, at that time, and period.

That same year, Sam after his betrothal to, he then married, the woman who would become his first wife, Verna Bey.

Verna and Sam met when both were thirteen years old. Verna or 'Mom Verna' as she is referred to, eventually and to this day, assumed and still holds to pretty much the highest degree and distinction, the role of, matriarch to all or most, of Sam's children.

With the 'conscious-raising' knowledge and awareness that he had attained through The Moors Science Temple and in addition to, the climate of changes that were brewing about and through- out the United States as well as, the Western civilization part of the world, one would think it only the natural order of things or that, to be expected of what Sam next did.

In 1966, after introducing Verna to the religion, Sam, then joined the Nation of Islam.

Founded in 1930, nine years before Sam's birth in Detroit Michigan by its founder, Wallace D. Fard Muhammad, the Nation of Islam was a religious and social organization and movement that sought and seek to improve the spiritual, mental, social and economic conditions of Blacks in America. Although considered by many because of this, to be a supremacist or anti-Semitic group, it is this writer's contention that, had it not been for the Nation of Islam, many of our 'so- called' leaders both, of color and non-color for civil and or human rights both then, and now, would not have the ability to enjoy the liberty of being so. And nor, would they have had the real right or real 'freedom' to do so, had it first not, and evermore, acknowledged the existence, struggles, sacrifices, worth's and respect of the 'Negro' or Black man without first thought being of, subjugation or 'lesser'.

Thinking about this, I find my mind going to what Sam had said in regard to, the spiritual connection of a woman. Both of these thoughts, had intertwined and congealed that acknowledgement then in my mind, of that period precipitated a longing or desire to know an answer to something.

The answer that I sought inside of my mind inheritably though, I had already both sub- and consciously knew the answer to, So, I guess more poignantly or exact, I just wanted to have heard it verbalized, reiterated or confirmed.

I had wanted to know, the mind-set of a people subjected to such horrendous and or that, particular subjugation. So too, did Sam. I further noted in my mind of how to me, it seemed sort of akin to in analogy of, that of 'a woman in an abusive relationship who inside prayed and finally fought, for it to get better.' To many people, especially at that time, the Nation of Islam had came sort of akin to, that of a mirror, friend or deserving suitor to the inner-spirit then stating that, 'You are better than, the tyranny that desires to mold, shape, portray or make you out to be'. It was to a great many of the subjugated, like, an epiphany or urgent and imperative realization that needed to be addressed and enacted upon, by the abused or aggrieved woman if, the abusive situation was to be made better or resolved.

Although not ultimately, seeking separation, but acknowledgement, recognition and inclusion in the rights afforded by the Declaration of Independence however, excised from main-stream society or, the 'Powers that be' because of this next thought, the Nation of Islam had at that time, and akin to that of, an abused woman who had tired of the abuses avowed, instilled, re-affirmed and advocated with action to the subjugated and abuser that, 'true peace could and would not come unless, true dialogue, understanding and resolve be established between the abuser and the abused' or, subjugated.

I'm also quite certain at this point as I sat next to him and, as he has echoed that Sam, would not and did not mind as I inject to you the reader as, this is mainly directed at the male population, that you may perchance, think of these times, concepts, mind-sets and analogies the next time you decide to refer to your fellow-man using the terms in a derisive manner that describe either, a female's genitals or that, for a female dog. On this point, I am reminded of something else that Sam had relayed to me that, I will possibly, echo again throughout this writing. On and regarding, life, "Everything is designed to send a message to the mind." He went on further in relaying that, "Man, means mind and that, Woman, means 'Womb of the mind'." Initially, this concept or, observation floated by me like, a feather then, it hit me like, that meteorite in Russia did as he off-handily, and leisurely added, "She gives birth to thought." The Nation of Islam to Sam as well others, at that time, was something that was sorely, desperately and really needed. Spiritually, that having never been one of those, a delineation that I had sought to use in this literary dis- simulation of the man to give an objective view of his make-up in totality, the timing at that point in history, was right for Sam despite whatever part he, or the others may have consciously assisted in it.

"Up close, Satan, the enemy of God and Man"

One of the precepts of being a member in the Nation of Islam was abstinence from the use of all intoxicants, mind-altering or illicit drugs. Never having to been at that time one, to engage, indulge in the use of any of those substances this further opened, the door for Sam to practice with fervency, the tenets and teachings of the Nation of Islam.

Again with focus on the problems of blacks in America, these teachings allowed Sam, to observe his own Philadelphia town that he had previously viewed, with different eyes. It had allowed him and like others also, to view the things that were rampant and prevalent, and spiraling quickly out of control. It had helped him and those again, like others also, to really see themselves. It had allowed him and those countless others, many to this day, this writer included, to see, and believe in what was possible. Among its members, and many of those from within the urban communities, it allowed people to feel a sense of pride and determination to help others.

It also allowed people, who could not formerly, to freely realize and achieve positive goals.

Finally, as for Sam, it was in joining the Nation of Islam where, he had re-channeled himself as, his convictions became geared towards something to fight for and against.

Also, when Sam joined the Nation of Islam, it was then that, many of the stories, rumors, fabrications, allegations, lies, legends and myths began to flourish of which, we will dispel, dissect and hopefully, lay to rest at the completion of this writing.

Sam's third job was with his father who, was a supervisor on the Schuylkill Expressway project.

Here, mainly amongst Sam's duties, were to keep clear the drainage lines that were dug, to permit clearance of the river in whatever particular area of the project that, they mayhap had been working at a particular time.

I think it also prudent at this point to state that, let not those incidents between Sam and his father shared to you the reader earlier, be an example of say, a strained, mis-communicated or misunderstood relationship between his father and Junior or, 'Junie'. As with his mother, Sam or 'Junie' loved, his father. Unknown to 'Junie' however, as he was summoned or referred to by his parents, his father, until his verbal revelation to Sam had long ago, since Sam's childhood, been seeking or sought out Sam's approval as well .

A foppish man himself, who regularly held card games in his home, Sam's father, although as proven, a constant and participating influence in Sam's life, and did not live with his wife or children the whole duration of their relationship, made this revelation to Sam years later.

That was when, as an adult, Sam had visited his father in prison.

He had been incarcerated there as a result of having, had shot a white woman.

Although the crime at the same time, shook and re-affirmed Sam's conviction to the core, he did not disappoint, disown, or let down his own father either. During the tearful meeting, he had told his father, that he had long ago, forgiven him for all the negative things that had transpired in their lives during the building of that or their, relationship. His father then in turn, let Sam who, had by this time, been assigned his 'X', (the removal of his government or given last name and the assignment of the unknown factor designated by the 'X' until an attribute was given) and thus, had become known as, Samuel 6X (the number designated the numerical order of the designee given the 'X' that bore the same first name) know, how happy he was that, Sam had embraced, and was clinging to his religion. Not digressing, or making concession for any of the things mentioned in this story, but some key observations must be pointed out at this juncture.

Organize, Deputize and Supervise

'It was time to get up off of the one knee.' In this regard, I am not stating, the 'One knee' meaning, the atrocities that blacks had suffered and are still suffering by, being beaten down from, and as a result of, the struggle to free themselves from the effects of forced slavery, bondage and servitude although they too, were factors that they also had to deal and contend with. In addition to their longing to be accepted as, 'Equals' in the quote, unquote mainstream society or scheme of it, it was also time to, get off the one knee of, 'acceptance'.

With that, I mean, acceptance of the one knee bent in a 'crap game' or, the bent knee of acceptance of the self-hate and denigration with-in one's self and from others of blacks, as being worthy of nothing more than, the nefarious things that they have chosen to accept or, what was imposed upon them. In this respect, many of the things that Sam's father and others like him, had, and were engaged in, fell into the realm of those incongruities to evince or, attest to the test of Sam's convictions.

*'A man convinced of his will against his will, will still be, of the
same opinion unless, he is made to see the error of his ways'*

**"I'm not going to let you, the prosecution stand in my court-
room and paint a picture of Al Capone and nor, am I going to let
you, the defense paint a picture of Robin Hood."**

Sam's first actual conviction in a court of law came as a result of,
what a large proportion of what many other youths suffered or suffer
from. It was another one of those terms or diagnosis coined by psychology. It was called, 'reactance'. And although psychology describes
it as, 'a response to, an authorities figure' i.e. parents, teachers what
have you, it means nothing more than what it says to, 'react'. The
contrast then, for Sam and others like him around that time however,
verses people of non-color then, and many of the youth today was
given, the temperament and acceptance of corporeal punishment as a
means to correct or effuse errant behavior against 'establishment' and
the proximity of the short period of time when others had begun the
fight to make it an illegal and unacceptable act to practice on people
of color made for a volatile contrasting of ideologies. For Sam's reactance, it first led to him being assigned to Boone. A disciplinarian
school, Boone was a 'last ditch' effort to prevent or, to prepare one,
for the transition to such places like, Glen Mills or say, 'The Youth
Study Center' or, the other residential or 'mini-prisons' in the city
for boys. Sleighton Farms had yet to have been developed for the girls.
Involved in a physical altercation with a teacher while at Boone, Sam
was then transferred to White Hill prison later named, Camp Hill
thus, missing those other youth centers or facilities altogether in the
expeditious process.

While there, and armed with books and the knowledge and com-
radeships that he had gained from Kenyatta and the Moor's Science
Temple Sam then, never lost his affinity for his South Philly roots as
at every turn, it seemed and appeared that he, in some form, fashion

or way sought out, gravitated to, and defended or protected or 'had the back' of anyone from there.

As it had been relayed to me from 'Brother Hamid' or, as is now, his attribute, Donnie Day, "Sam was no physically big dude. He just had this swagger and assurance about his self as, he'd walk down the center of the halls, walkways and through the yard throughout the compound"

"Yo, you need to tell your man to Break down on that Bop!"

Here, at this point, Donny demonstrates to me, the certain way that Sam would wear his facility issued woolen hat while there. Putting the two pictures together in my mind, and learning of his loyalty and dedication to his fellow-South Philadelphians, I am instantaneously forced and compelled to agree with his next statement as he then says, "When you saw him, you were first forced to admire and then ultimately, respect him." For emphasis, he then adds, "You couldn't help it, but to!" He then, for the time being, concludes by telling me, "He wasn't loud or boisterous or anything like that."

As it was also relayed to me, from Brother Karim or Russell Morgan, "If he were in a room with ten other people, you wouldn't know which one was him. He wasn't loud or flashy or any of that stuff, that you would expect or see in other cats."

Whether, he was aware of the respect and admiration that his persona commanded, I would be doing he, myself and you, a disservice in attempting to discern. However, I will with certainty, venture to state that, at White Hill, he had to be aware of, the power of unity that he had, or could meld or bring together. And upon his release, that is exactly, what he had then set out to do. Now, of the rumors that I was privy to have heard, one in particular, I had found, as I had wanted to believe was true, as I had heard it repetitively both, from intimates in the closest of his circle as well as those, outside of it and of those, having never really had the opportunity of meeting him alike. That one was, of a certain street corner in South Philly.

There, it was where strangers from the most indigent to junkies alike met, and would congregate on many Saturday mornings to lay in wait for Sam. What I had found amusing about this certain story was, as it had also been relayed to me, about the despondency, dismay, shock and almost terrifying fear and dread when he would miss making that meeting on some Saturday mornings. This was because while there, he would attempt without warrant, worry or memory of whom, to fulfill every monetary request of those gathered there, that had been waiting for him.

Here, I must inject one his delineations passages or responses to, in regard to my central query of characteristics and traits in regard to my point on convictions, or more pointedly his, in describing this observation or rumor. On Loyalty, "To be dedicated to a cause greater than yourself. To exemplify a willingness to sacrifice to a cause other than one's self"

There was also, another one of those things, that I had heard resounded in regard to Sam.

Fabled, and then finally affirmed through him, he was said by others first, to have said on a many occasions, "I never desired to be a leader. I just wanted, enjoyed and was comfortable being a soldier."

There was something else too, that had been relayed to me by others, and thus, again reaafirmed by him. As our eyes met on this particular day, it was being resonated yet once again as we all, he and I, and those particular others who, were sitting together at this particular time.

Rest assure also, it will be resonated again in this dissection for dissemination and hopefully, ultimate dissertation to appease one's desire, interest, thirst or quest to learn of, and quell those wants in regard to this man, and the rumors, allegations and tales of legend associated with him.

"We weren't bad people. We were sincere people whose sincerity was misused and abused."

I inject this assertion now, for the thoughts and wonders that have plagued the minds of the, just wanting to quench a thirst for something akin to that, of a pulp fiction novel in the library or dime store. For, we will, address those thirsts with specification.

Now, to exemplify how, this assertion could be applied to practically any, or every one.

Also, although again as it will be resonated throughout, it is injected again to put forth the question that, 'given the gravity of the things associated with this particular individual' and, the situations surrounding same, 'if put in the same situation, would another's conviction or faith be wavered?' For the sake of objectivity and integrity I must also now, inject a perception, inference or judgment that a great number of people may no doubt concur with. I myself both, from personal experience as well as, deductive reasoning have to, and must also concur with that perception. I know these two facts to be certain and of the main precipitant for the rightful bolstering of the validity for this inference. This is because, with hind-sight bias, even Sam was forced, compelled or, of his own volition, to concur with it.

This objective personal perception, inference or judgment is that, 'although initially, a noble much worthy cause when he, and the like-minded others with him, had embarked upon to make change, they had done so, engaging in a war that was so deceptive, toxic and vicious that they, like others before or since, have been unable to win'.

Whether, by poetic design or, just the simple resultant, the opposing force was, has been, and is now, so inebriating and ruefully destructive that it has, and still consumes nations.

This enemy, Sam nor, the others before or since, has been or is now, exempted from as it has ultimately in the end, consumed most in one fashion or another.

This mighty enemy was and is now called, power, destitution, treachery, greed and iniquity.

Once again, initially a noble and oft-said, 'novel' idea. However, remember, 'A man convinced against his will,'. The war, that they had embarked upon was in all essence, 'A fool's war'. 'To control a man's thoughts, desires and wants makes all else ease.'

At the risk, and necessity of breaking away from the populace of that perception and yet still towards, and for integrity and objectivity, I would like to offer up my own little expository.

Majority of people as a whole, let alone a race of people, 'we don't own on a regular basis, planes or ships designed or equipped for transport of, one of the main weapons or proponents that enables or assists the perpetual victory of that, or those enemies'. This does not negate however, the responsibility that, that fact aside as people, we retain, as is our rights, duties and ownership for the choices we make.

During this period, as with the present day, when the proponent of drugs have been, and are injected into the equation, this makes all other opposing alternatives or objectives extremely difficult if not altogether mute, or 'moot' to that sought, to be opposed.

Initially, with the most ardent religious fervency, this and the destructive results of it, is what Sam, and those like-minded others, had sought to allay or alleviate. "The Bible and the Quran do not contradict each other. When man injects his opinion, it enables and causes confusion." was one of the first things that, Sam had relayed to me.

Re-affirming yet once again, of how deep, of an opportunity that I have been given was, what he had then said, and later went on to both verbally, and chronologically evince. He went on verbally at first in stating, and thus, having the where-with-all, courage and knowledge to admitting and again conceding that, despite or in spite of one's religion and their, stead-fastness to it, that the enemies or destructive oppositions to it, were comparably at times, much stronger evincing to, the separatism of God, 'power' and man. He did this in his, expressing his own, up close and personal experiences and such. And again, as you will see, it was and is, quite an experience.

In this world today, how many are there, that are standing on, or profess to standing strong on constitution and conviction that can or are, willing to admit, or to say that, "Yes I have, in the interim of loving God, lain and lusted with Satan"? That list I wager, would not be a very long one. Not since, the many times that I hear people say, "I'm saved!" or, they are portraying the image of piety after or, in the interim between dwelling in dens or situations of iniquity and evil. That's one of those funny things about people in as how, 'they seem to, develop selective amnesia when they want to as if, the life that they had lived before their metamorphous or, finding religion never happened.'

'A trying World full of Sinners.'

And good gracious, were there some challenges awaiting Sam and the others too!

What 'Twist' or 'Spin' of the 'left', could I put on this very important part of this story, that cannot today, be added or inferred up to anything more than, 'Different' names, but same 'Lames' and 'lanes' of expectations placed before men of color from very start of the word, 'hello'. Before I continue on though, I must stop to relay a couple of things that happened at this juncture of my gathering information from Sam for the writing of this or his, autobiographical documentary.

We were out one day, as what had become our norm' for our early morning regiment of exercise, enlightenment and edifying when all of a sudden, from up above us as we had stopped on a street corner, there was this lady that yelled down in earnest, "Hey you, don't you move! If you move, I'll throw this pot of hot grease down on you! You're Sam Christian! You're Sam Christian right?"

After he politely answered up to her in the affirmative, she then added, as it sounded like she was saying it with her breath held and heart stopped, "Don't you move! I'll be right down there!"

For promise and emphasis she added one more time, "I coming right down there, now!"

As she left the window with a barely discernible trace of a grin, I knew that, she was another one of those people that I had and would be meeting along the way in my, journey, coming down with a tale of pride and proudness to convey to, and of Sam. At that moment she, and like those others that I had met and would meet, did not know that, I was there in the capacity of the writer of his autobiography. Nor, did Sam reveal this fact to her until upon, the ending of this particular story of her, in-particular tale or 'happening'. She then went on to relay that once, when she was about eight-teen years old back in the 70's, she had run away from home. She relayed to us of how, she had happened upon Sam driving, a red Cadillac and him seeing her this one night/early morning.

Although as she recalled to, having remembered to, "had just turned eighteen at the time," she conceded too that, just turned eight-teen at the time, she conceded too that, she remembered still being, or having to have looked, out of place in that certain place, and at so un-godly an hour, as that it was more closely to having been, in the early wee-twilight hours of this particular morning'.

"You came by me and asked me what I was doing out there. You then, asked me did I need a ride any place. I didn't have any place to go. And you rode me around all night. You didn't do nothing to me and you didn't ask for sex or anything like that. Nope, you just rode me around until it started to get light outside in the morning. You then went and bought me a whole new outfit, and gave me fifty dollars." I know, what you, the reader may be thinking about here as, did I before, a quick recall in my mind of Sam's, 'Booster', friends.

"You then asked me did I want to be dropped off somewhere or did I have a place to go. Then, you dropped me off on my street and told me to take care and be safe. I never forgot that, Yup."

And like her, as he often inquired of her, as we passed by that particular area, I felt compelled to write or relay this particular event to you because of two things. One is because, every so often as I would be gaining information and writing, it would slip from my mind as to who, it is that I was writing about, and walking with. I guess this was in part because, as I have stated, the kinship, friendship and brotherhood that we have forged or that, had been melded together along the way, and because of it. Then there was number two that, because of that particular happening, and the assuredness or expectation of many more like it to come, I would, and had never forget that particular one.

The other 'happening' personally to me, which I wanted to share as again, I had been out one day, walking and absorbing from Sam was, of some inter-turmoil that had been festering and building inside of me, at that particular juncture or, time. I had been carrying this thing around inside of my very own self and for a very long time too. I am going to presume it not warranted any longer to expound on that, and once again as it would be, that it was in observing, and gathering from him that, that moment of revelation or observation was observed.

I had been deeply irked as of late as, I thought in regard to him like, that Harold Melvin and The Blue Notes song had lamented, "Where have all my friends gone?" One of the brothers had failed to make good on a promise that he had made to Sam. This failure, had really affected me deeply.

As I was to learn, it not only affected me in a way that it should not have and that, it took me to places that I need not have, or had been in my mind. But it did not, as so, it should not had or have affected Sam in the least. This incident, or thing granted by a power that I could not explain or comprehend then, granted him the freedom and leeway in his sphere, and again, probably un-knowingly and too, probably unconcernedly in his mind, to grant to me finally, some solace and peace in my own heart and mind from his, wisdom, knowledge and aura. Witnessing the trace physical effects and toll that this broken promise (at least, that's how I saw it in my mind,) as it, had been taking on me, with the redness of useless frustration contrasted by the bloated state of the distended veins coursing my cervix and appendages he leaned over to me and asked truly concerned, "Are you bothered because that brother, did not show up?" After I had answered in the affirmative, he then asked, "What did he say happened?" to which, I responded, "He said, he was in a meeting." "Well, why can't you believe that he was? Allah, is the knower of all things." I then felt, comfortable and comforted enough to impart to him that, "Brother Beyah, all my life I've had this trouble with forgiveness." After imparting to me several examples he then goes on in stating that, "Allah's mercy supersedes his wrath". He then went on, and stated to me, "If you want to forgive someone, you must first asked Allah to help you. Then when you say you forgive, you must really do so in, never back-biting or mentioning the matter again. Remember too, that what you say, Allah hears. So, don't say it unless you really mean it."

With that, he then lifted me up in a way that, I would have never thought possible upon sharing this knowledge with me as, I truly then for probably, the first time in my life, began letting go of the weight of that burden and all of the other things that had been weighing me down throughout my whole life to free itself, from my psyche and soul. It was also then, and because of that, that I had truly made for the first time, an avowal to, 'from that point on' to, practice in earnest that lesson that he had both, unknowingly and knowingly imparted upon me. I would ever-more concentrate on forgiveness of the adversities that I had felt, have or had been committed upon, or against me.

I realized then, at that point, that I had really not grasped and or, applied any of those lessons that I had thought or professed, that I had a grasped in my previous book.

Before I go back to the challenges that had awaited Sam, I want to add one more piece of valuable knowledge that he had stated, that was re-iterated and evinced in this certain incident. He had said, "Sometimes, you never know, the man you may be looking for, may be looking for you to help you." And here it was, as I was thinking that, it was I who, were the one, in the position of administering the most help. Yet, once again, 'an older version of the powerful man that he is,' and or, was.

The 'Left' as I had alluded to previously is, with emphasis on being, or falling 'behind' in regard to equality. There, there were as usual, the usual suspects and its victims. The suspects as usual were, the drugs, the gambling and prostitution top amongst the many other 'traps' or, the likes. The victims are, and were as will be, the offspring of ignorance. Of them, they are then cast about into a world of mixed signals sprinkled through with a vast amount of soul-stealing, soul-selling affinities to further enrapture away from, or 'enslave' the knowledge of one's true self or worth.

Of that world, pour in just a dash more of ignorance and a few slight variances of name or term of the 'new' iniquitous or (ies) and then one would have, a more empathetic and commiserating view of what obstacles men (and women) of color mostly, as well as others, had and have to contend with, navigate and endure as we were then, coming out of that certain period or point in time. Then imagine, all of the strings or variables leading back into a circle that is ultimately manipulated and controlled by someone else that has obtained it and holds it illegally. Then imagine that same someone, repeatedly and with mind-boggling (il) or, logic justifying to you, that you have no stake in prospering let alone, surviving, or living in it. Then, you would still not have even a minuscule of the plight before a passenger or descendent of or, on that fateful passage courtesy of greed and wretchedness called, and specifically, 'The Middle Passage'.

Then, enter, the real 'Men in Black' or, suits. Again, with no malicious or jealous slight towards Will Smith, but thank you very much! Predicated or instilled from the teachings and principles of the honorable Elijah Muhammad, Sam once relayed to me that, the honorable Elijah Muhammad had incorporated the idea of putting the Nation of Islam members into uniforms from, Marcus Garvey.

Marcus Mosiah Garvey, known for his activism, Black Nationalism and Pan-Africanism in 1919, he tried to persuade the government of Liberia to grant land on which black people from America could settle. Until the male members of the Nation of Islam were bestowed or granted the opportunity to wear one of those uniforms thus then, becoming known as, one of the 'Fruits of Islam', they would mainly be adorned in a black or inconspicuous dark suit hence, the term, 'Men in Black suits' in response to, or in case, the people or writers behind, one of those "expose's" should have the notion that, 'We don't, or have not done our research". We heard you!

I, after a series of some serious observations as well as, careful considerations and conversations have concluded that, the number one reason for the public notification of Sam Christian or, of his presence to the public outside of the Nation of Islam yet while, in regard and because of it, was none other than, 'The Greatest of All Time!', Muhammad Ali, himself.

"He was the number one reason why, I became the number one, and top seller of newspapers in Philadelphia!" he told me, one day. The newspaper he is referring to was called at that time, 'Muhammad Speaks' later re-named, 'The Final Call'. Once again, with this, I was reminded of the little adage that he threw out there saying," You never know, the man you may be looking for,".

"He walked all the way with me, from 22nd & South to the Water front." The Water front that he was referring to is, the Delaware River or 'Penn's Landing'. And if you're from the City of Brotherly Love, you would know what he is saying and means by that, as it is, a very long walk. However, that walk nor, the reasons for it, were much of a chore for the champ. "Everyone wanted to meet him, white people included." 22nd & South is the place that Sam, with all of his heart claims, to be his first hangout, 'corner' or, 'headquarters'. I recently heard another guy and Sam speaking about something that guys from that particular part of town, used to do with their Stacy's

(Stacy Adams shoes) that, I am anticipating doing when I get my next pair. As the guy began, "We, used to take baking soda and mix it up with water, then, with a toothbrush, apply it to the white stitching." At this, Sam interjected and finished with, "Yeah, and rub it on the white stitching to take off the wax and bring back the gloss of the white stitching on the sides of them." These are South Philly guys whom I've always heralded as, 'the Kings of Style!' These were the 'tailor-made' guys!

I, in meaning, real tailors that, a great number of the guys from South Philly were. They were, as Donny Day exclaimed, "the pioneers of fashion" in, Philly. Also again, and this was the same man that would eventually, do away with gangs 'per say all through-out all of Philadelphia.

The hate that, hate produced.

At the time of its inception when it was formed, the Nation of Islam's main and crowning objective was to, 'unite and empower' a people on, the precipice of uncertainty in both, future and direction who were, in the beginning stages of finding freedom from slavery. Being one of the first up-front action for action organizations in North America whose again, crowning and main objectives were to first and foremost, have that freedom recognized and honored for the so called, African-American Negro in that America and at that time. On the opposing side at that time, was the realization yet, unwillingness to relent to this objective. Willing, that opposition was not, to the abolishment of the free indentured servitude based solely, and sovereignly on the origin and color of a people here also solely, as a result of that 'Middle Passage' that, was touched upon briefly earlier. Naturally, as a result of self-preservation, nor, were they open to releasing that bondage or binds with any sense of, or towards equality and, still yet to be recognized fully, but also especially at that time, forget about reparations.

This was the same hate that, produced such other notable people as say, Frederick Douglas, Harriet Tubman, Sojourner Truth, Nat Turner and Malcom X to name a few.

With these obstacles built up against blacks at the time, the chore of the Nation of Islam was to, (re) or instill a love of self for the black man and woman in America. In doing so, and as, an anecdote for the self-hate that was accepted or instilled too, did they preach, teach or implore eradication of the love for the enemy that had caused that self-hate. It was already inheritably apparent that, the underlying root for that initial hate was the result of differences in first, color and then the other ephemeral and common things. So, that made the latter (the ephemeral and common things) of least importance and minute in regard to, the whole over-all scheme of the big picture. Yes, that was minute. It was about equality and equal treatment in thereof.

All the way from the prophets and the martyrs of the present day, it was about equality for all men. Instilled and inbred, this is how that reactance to that hate, that produced hate was born.

It was that, to Sam and the many others at that time that, was the precipitant for the rift or so called, 'war' between the races in Northern America also around, that time. It was built on the fear of one race of people against another, which had been previously held in bondage by the former of the two. Naturally, though need not being said, the emphatic desire and extents of both forces to have their point of view validated can, could and did go beyond an expected and oft-times un-imaginable and un-explainable level to be manifested and realized. A 'hell' of a time and predicament to be in as any, and many would agree.

Yet and still, as Sam was wont to say, 'sometimes, drastic changes call for, drastic measures and just as drastic changes'. The work and constitution to accomplish these things too sometimes, called for one, with or without a 'conscience' once again, 'in the vain, crass and ubiq-uitous sense of the term' to enact these changes. As will be evinced, and this is where Sam or, 'The Top of the Clock' would prove worthy, or adept for the chore. I had recently heard it relayed by one of the brothers who had formerly, been under the command of Sam when he was promoted to the rank of lieutenant thus becoming, 'Lieutenant Samuel 6 X' that he, had once heard it echoed in another city in regard to Temple No. 12 or, 'The Top of the Clock' as they were called that, "When it comes to the profession, leave the profession to the professional!" Forgive me if you must, but I have taken the liberty in naming them to, the total summation of character attributes I or, another may think required for the type of individual 'tapped' or, enlisted, for the assignment that was required thus, 'The Professionals'.

I am again reminded at this point, of another conversation that I once, had with Sam in regard to, the way and why, he had chosen to speak about, a lot of the things that we had, or would be speaking and writing about in military terms. The older version of the powerful man, then with a direct stare that left no distinction between the 'now' and 'former' zeroed in on me, with pinpoint and most-assuredly radar-like, not to be disputed accuracy and stated, "Because, that's what it was! A war. We were, in a war. That's what it was." Again, that's why the brothers at Mosque number 12 were called, 'The Professionals'.

And so, after having myself, had spent some time in the Military thus, granting me an awareness of Sam's mind-set and reasoning in this regard, I have taken the liberty in naming the analogy or comparison to, giving the chore and plight that lay ahead of them to that, and using a military term or operation, but with a different connotation, 'the Black Ops' or 'Special Forces'. Again, that's why the brothers at Mosque number 12 were, and as I having chosen to address them as such called, 'The Professionals'.

Actually, and according to Sam as, I am no doubt inclined to agree with, they were the vanguard (the leading party or persons in a movement) for, the 'First Resurrection'. As revealed to me by Sam, and confirmed by others, the 'First Resurrection' was the response of hate in return for, the fear and hate practiced against, and of, the passengers and their descendants of the Middle Passage that by proclamation, were supposedly considered, to be free.

"You are beautiful!" was the word of the day. As I've stated earlier, several thoughts or sentiments would be echoed throughout this writing. One in particular, which is resounding now, is the one about, 'a man convinced of his will against his will,'.

That sentiment in case, it should have been missed or now, needs to be re-iterated was, not only in regard to the people or, 'fish'. That sentiment also applied in regard to, a many of the number of the brothers and sisters or 'recruited' that were enlisted, in the Nation of Islam as well.

Before we expound on that point though, I'd like to now, place focus on a number of the things that they had sought to oppose or allay on, or en-route to, that realization or 'awakening'.

First thing on the agenda was, to 'eliminate the psychological power or hold of a 'Spook-God' or the Michael Angelo depiction of our so called, 'Savior'.' One in-particular jocular sentiment or delineation that I have heard Sam and several others from the first resurrection in analogy to exemplify the imperativeness of addressing number one on the agenda was, in the way of song.

In using that analogy, they no doubt, had as the aim, to go directly to the heart. Before I expound on that analogy, I wish now to add something that I'd came upon in a psychology book somewhere along in my travels in life. In this book it stated that, the number one and two reasons or causes for prejudice in the world are, the scarcity of resources and religion.

Now, to the analogy used by Sam and a number of the others. "Have you really ever listened to church or 'gospel' music? Did you ever listen to the music that was emanated from the black churches? And did you ever listen to the music that was emanated from the white churches? What do they be singing or saying in the black churches? They be lamenting about, 'hang on in there, Christian soldier,' or, 'when our lord comes back to get us'. What do they be exclaiming and singing about in those white churches? They be talking about, 'Fight on, Christian soldier!' or, 'With the sword of my lord!' "

Portrayed, before the audience of the world as, the 'most abominable and sub-species of human', the Nation of Islam was, one of the first up-front action-for-action organizations in North America for the blacks of America turned, and with loud verbal reverberation retorted that, "No! You, are the devil!" This, was a long time before, "Say it loud!" became the word, catch-phrase and sentiment of a revolution.

And, the loyalty of these two opposing forces ran deep and very loyal to their perspective points of view. Hence, these reason why I placed the emphasis on, 'white people included,' when I wrote in regard to the Champ and Sam.

Speaking of the Champ, later, when Sam makes his decision to embrace 'True Islam', several things about the Champ that Sam had witnessed that, I will now mention, would be a major precipitant in that decision. True as it may have been that, Tom Levin and the South Philadelphia that Sam had been reared in may have been 'tailored-made' so that he had never, had to look out at the things that existed or was coming in the ensuing storm.

However, things did transpire or happen and, he did look, and again, they did happen. There it was, the whole story in black and white and in a 'nut-shell' well, sort of.

Still aware of where, you the reader, wants to venture to and as, we are going to get there, we have decided that it be most prudent that, we give it to you in its entirety. While reflecting on the time that Sam had spent with the Champ, he expressed to me a number of things that dropped my jaws, wowed me and ultimately, wowed me again and then, blew me away.

Starting from the latter because, everything culminating to it in itself, seemed to be, unable to be matched. He blew me away when he said that, "Muhammad Ali changed the whole concept of black and white thinking." Floored, I asked him to elaborate on that. But, before we do get to Sam's elaboration, I'd like to bring out something else, that we had touched upon in the process of gathering information for his story. I had mentioned to Sam that, upon reading some excerpts from his story, that some of the readers stated that, although they feel as that it is a very good story and, it is being told in a concise and correct manner, they also felt, as if the word usage and vocabulary is one, that makes them feel as if they have to keep a dictionary present by their sides while doing i.e., the dissecting and reading this story.

I then relayed to him, that as a writer, one of my most personal objectives is to do just that. I do this because, I feel very strongly and deeply inside that as a people, this is where we fall short as in, our efforts to have seriously and sincerely communicated, or gain the ability to make known truly, our needs, rights and demands as a people. I think that we spend too much time and thought in building, and having a sub-cultural accepted while, we gripe and complain about that which, of our own choosing, we resignedly accept as 'just the way things are' when it comes to our government.

Nelson Mandela once said, "In order to understand the government that I was seeking to change, I felt it imperative that I first, learned the language of that government" (to secure one's freedom from his captor) In addition to psychology's over-all concurrence to this fact, this he did to, the fear and dismay of one of his associates or fellow South Africans.

Communication being a two-way street, I feel it imperative that one at least, make an attempt to learn or familiarize themselves with some lingual semblance of the party that he or she is communicating with, about a need. However, as a people, we seemingly, find it more imperative that we learn the language of the day, as in, I mean, that in the most ephemeral sense of the term than to, put the effort in to understanding the basic rules of and to, the 'game' of this Western civilization society and its culture.

And there, as once again psychology has stated, I believe, it starts with one's ability to understand, grasp and communicate in the language of that society. The ability to truly, communicate equals, the ability to be truly understood. On that note, and finally, as to my most staunch and ardent reason for doing this, 'Once you have not the knowledge, but the ability to know where to seek out information to grasp an understanding of a word or situation then, you have the ability to unlock doors and thirst for greater things."

So, for that reason, as Sam has concurred, "One should always seek to broaden their vocabulary as that, broadens their minds." I shall continue on, as I have been, and hope that you will, with me. If the need arises, please feel free to as, I have and do, utilize your dictionary if you will hopefully, become further enlightened in not just the understanding of this man's story, but the ability to sincerely, communicate yours, or your needs, wants and desires as well.

When I asked Sam to elaborate on how, 'The Greatest of All Time' had changed the concept of black and white thinking, what he stated to me came like first, a blast from a double-barreled shot gun with the purpose of to, give instead of taking life, new found thoughts, whose explosions of enlightenment were like, one of those fourth of July fireworks displays with, the different array of colors and seemingly endless succession of explosions.

In my mind, the succeeding explosions were like, masses of newly found perspectives or dazzling lights of valuable information. It felt sort of akin to me like, a new world opening up, if you will.

He said to me that, "Ali killed racism in Elvis Presley and Elvis in turn, killed racism in me." He went on in saying, "After he did that, he opened my liking, and ear up to other white artists. He was the reason, that I started liking Frank Sinatra and Tony Bennett and other white music."

Not only with a 'Whoa', but with a great resounding 'Wow!' one, would have to admit that, being what Sam was and involved in around that time that, was a lot of racism that had to be killed. I venture too, that this was around about the time, that things started to change once again in Sam's life. But we will, as stated, go through and get to that point in the story as well.

I then went on in, asking him how, The Champ had accomplished this task. Before he went on in explaining how, he first went on in stating, "Muhammad Ali was responsible for changing not only Elvis Presley's thinking towards the black man, but he was also responsible for, bringing a lot of white people to Islam."

Of course, everyone remembers in January, 1973 when Muhammad Ali was readying to fight Joe Bugner or, (Aussie Joe) as was his professional pugilistic moniker on February 14 right? He, Muhammad Ali and Elvis unknown to each other, had admiration for each other in their perspective talents. After initially meeting each other, and each again, looking and taking in each other like one would, if in the presence of, or viewing the Mona Lisa, Elvis had then, adjourned back to his hotel room.

Upon returning, he then presented, 'The Champ', Muhammad Ali with a specially made for the 'Champ' fifty-thousand dollar bejeweled silk robe with an inscription on the back that read, 'The People's Champ'.

The Champ then eventually, returns the favor as, he invites Elvis up to his training camp in Dear Lake, Pennsylvania and, the two build a friendship that has lasted ever since up until the time of Elvis's death. On Vegas though, I imagine that, that must have been one meeting worth not only seeing, but paying to see, in the energy with Elvis being surrounded on his one side by, his white entourage and Muhammad Ali being surrounded on his by, the Nation of Islam and seeing both of those groups, being eclipsed by the men that they, were there to serve.

I had become even more astounded to learn that, three years ear-lier, Sam had been in attendance at Muhammad Ali's October 26th, 1970 fight against Jerry Quarry in Atlanta. This was the same year and approximately one month after, Sam 'Bam' Cunningham trounced over the Crimson Tide and through the walls of racism, in America.

Looking back in history; although that latter fact may seem, a thing that may pale in comparison to the former, and not something quite worthy of remembrance in regard to the whole over-all context of this particular man's story, but giving also the fact that, this is a story and about in particular too, racism and not just one of, someone sitting around simply talking or chewing the fat, it may seem not so inconsequential a thing, worthy of mentioning.

But, back to, and in regard to Sam, what is, and of intricate and monumental importance worth mentioning is the reason why, Sam had been in attendance at that particular fight. The reason why Sam had been in attendance at that particular fight was because, he had been enlisted by one, Captain Yusuf (first East Coast Regional Captain of the Nation of Islam) as the head, of security for 'The Champ' for that particular fight.

That particular fight with Jerry Quarry where Sam, was enlisted as head of the 'Champ's' security was, Muhammad Ali's first fight after being re-instated into boxing by the United States Supreme Court and the boxing commission after his refusal, to be drafted in the United States Military Service.

Sam's relationship with Muhammad Ali was not unlike, that of Elvis's and the 'Champ's' as his, and 'The Champ's' became an ami-cable and a lasting one, as well.

I've even heard that, since being with Sam where, others from time to time call him, 'The Champ' although, they were for different reasons of which, we will again as promised, touch upon later.

He also, used to attend and just 'hang out' at 'The People's Champ's' training camp there, in Dear Lake just up past Interstate 76 away from Philly, a way's past of course. The reason why I have placed the emphasis on 'hang out' in Sam's regard and Muhammad's training camp is because of a few things that he had mentioned to me about when and while he was, 'hanging out', there.

With great emphasis he expresses to me, "Ali, used to run like a deer!" With equal emphasis he then adds, "Just when you'd think he'd be tiring, he would be just getting his second wind."

He understands my laughter and imagining, as he tells me of the time when he thought he could hang with him while he, (Ali) was doing his road work or run. "Man, I remember this one time, when he had ran so far, that I got tired." The emphasis, that he had placed on 'tired' sounded as if, he had just finished that run. "Man, I was so tired, that I ran to the side of the road. And after I bent over and got my wind back, I walked to the nearest restaurant and called a cab to take me back to camp."

At this, I burst out in laughter. "Now, Jahbar, could hang with him! Them, two, used to spar all the time!" Jahbar, that he is referring to here is, Robert 'Nudie' Mims. Now, one may recall or have some knowledge of 'Nudie' if they can recall, that fire that took place at one, Dubrow's Furniture store in South Philadelphia.

He then goes on in stating, "That's why the Honorable Elijah Muhammad named him, 'Allah's Champion' for the people, because he was a Champion for all men. He was a beautiful brother. You couldn't help but to love him. He made everyone that he met, feel the love for him. That included both, blacks and whites, stranger or friend, he made everyone that he met, feel special."

I then, concluded here, for the time being when, I asked him, "How did he refer to you? Did he call you Sam or Beyah?"

"No, no. He called me brother. He called everyone he met either, brother or sister." He then, goes on to give me a little imitation of how Muhammad Ali sounded as he went on, "He would be like, 'Uh, hey brother' or, 'Come on over here brother'". In addition to, not being able to help but smile, I couldn't help but imagining, as I closed my eyes and I could actually hear, 'The Champ' with his soft spoken and comforting voice. That is, or was, the other voice when, he was not spouting off with his dead-on predictions that earned him the moniker, 'The Louisville Lip'. I also, added this because, I would have never imagined in a million years that, Sam Christian could be quite the mimic too. In other words to me and, this is just my own personal self, a person that could take a stab at imitating someone else also, has to be a person equipped with, not only the ability, but some semblance or retention of a soul, keeping in mind, the mindless monster that some people have made Sam, out to be.

Also, before leaving this particular point, I also know personally and unequivocally that, Sam cannot hold a note in song. I can say that as, it has been evinced when, we would be messing around and just playing with my music and stereo that was equipped with a microphone. But they did not stop him from singing anyway and, he did not mind laughing at himself or, that inability. Just more stuff I found out about the, 'Mindless Monster' that many again, have made him out to be.

As it is also known, the list of prominent people that Sam knew, or had in some form or another, interacted with, did not just extend to personalities out in some different stratosphere as he tells me of a meeting he once had, with a local radio personality in his Philadelphia.

Once, at the behest of the then minister at that time, of Mosque number 12, Jeremiah Shabazz, Sam was sent to see Mary Mason, a popular radio personality at the radio station that she broadcasted from (maybe, you've heard of it, it's call letters were W.H.A.T?) in regard to, some statements that she had made on air.

Part of Jeremiah's reasoning for doing such, may have had played some part because, Sam and Mary had sort of a history together, if you will.

Sam's aunt and his mother's eldest sister(Sam's mother was next behind her), Elsie Riles was in addition to, a very close friend of Mary's but also, used to care for Mary's son, Steven.

Sam and Mary Mason were so close that, she used to call him, 'Junie' just like, his mother used to. Now, Junie was not the name that Sam, just let any and every one call him by on a regular, friendly and or, free basis.

He in turn, used to call her, 'Aunt Mary'. Upon theirs, and this particular meeting though, it was stated to Mary that, she had or, was heard to have made some rather harsh, disparaging and seemingly, rash statements expressing, her personal disdain and aversions against the Nation of Islam. Mary Mason whom, had a fairly broad and expansive fan-base that spread across vast, and different ethnic and racial lines was however, staunch in her conviction of not discriminating against people of any color and she had no qualms nor trepidations about, expressing this fact so, and to, whomever. Although Sam already knew this, after expressing this to him, and reaffirming that she had nothing against the Nation of Islam, she had even went so further as to, agree to a personal meeting with Jeremiah himself. At the end of the meeting with her convictions still intact, it had been concluded that, she had been misquoted or, what she had been heard to have said, was taken out of context in what was broadcasted.

Another avid Muhammad Ali fan (and once a sportscaster according to Sam), Mary was then, courtesy of Sam, granted the opportunity to meet and have taken with Sam included in it, a picture of 'The Champ' himself.

She was then given the autographed picture of him that was delivered to her by again, Sam himself. Also, after this, and again, courtesy of Sam, she was then, one of the first visitors to the then new, 'Bilal Gardens' restaurant and treated to 'W.H.A.T' she then described as, "The best meal that, I had ever tasted!" Bilal Gardens was owned and managed by, Abu Bakkar and his wife.

Abu Bakkar had been known as before, adopting the name or, his

Muslim attribute as one, Eugene 'Bo' Baynes. In addition to 'Junie', she also at times, referred to him from time to time as, 'nephew'.

In regard to Mary, to Sam, she was likened to that which, Muhammad Ali (The Champ) was to him. She was, despite what many people's deep-seeded social perceptions may have been, or be about her, a 'Champion' in her own caring, and what she had did back then, for people as a whole.

The response to two, of the eleven attributes or delineations that I had initially in mind, come to me now as, I think about Sam in regard to his time with the Nation of Islam.

Those two attributes or delineations were with regard to, loyalty and conviction.

As we had touched upon earlier, his response to the question of what loyalty had meant to him was as follows, "To be dedicated to a cause greater than yourself. Expressing and exemplifying a willingness to sacrifice to a cause other than, one's own self."

In his response to the one on conviction, he had stated, "Serve God as though, you see him and know that, if you don't see him, he sees you. Have faith in God, in his servants, messengers and his prophets. If you get lost from that, then, you are truly lost like, a blind man roaming about in the dark."

This thought presently now, also brings to mind, something else that Sam had said to me in regard to the youth. "So, even if a man goes astray, know that, if Allah sees them worthy of repentance then, we as people should not turn our backs on them." In mentioning this last part, it is not done so again now, as a form or way of asking your forgiveness for any of the things that had transpired once again, in his life. But rather, it was meant, and mentioned at this point to evince or show, as imperative, the reasoning for some of the things that we are about to recall or relay.

Also, at this point, in regard to a lot of the things that were and are, taking place within the black communities, there was really again, not much distinction between the manner that a lot of adult people were, and are still, doing and accepting of things in ways that, would normally be expected of the youth.

In Philly, still once again, despite all that would eventually happen, Sam would make indelible impressions and changes into them both, the youths and the adult. So indelible an impression would he make into the former of those two, that one could unarguably assert that, it will ever-more play a part in the mind-set of its subcultural or the representatives of those that, many, will be participants in the reactance proportion of their numbers. I add this not, to glamorize or enamor this fact, but to evince to the proportional numbers of the latter in both, the home front and society as a whole, in the importance of being honest and consistent in the signals and messages that they or we, sincerely wish, to relay to the former.

So, Sam and this, Nation of Islam were ranting and preaching this thing about, 'the white man is the devil.' who cares? We had been bombarded with this God and devil dribble our whole lives in church without actually, seeing the physical presence of either. However, we were still feeling the 'physical' effects of, the physical 'hell' that was before us, in this existential 'white man's heaven' and 'black man's hell'. In that, I'm speaking about the unfair, disparaging, disproportionate, and different practices, standards and limits put before the people of color, in regard to living, working and education conditions. However too, keep in mind that now, this does not negate the way and reasons for the way that many of us waste, and treat irresponsive the miniscule opportunities that we have been given like for instance, welfare (titled initially by the Roosevelt administration, 'The Alms Act) and education.

Couple this in more intimately with, the castration, ostracizing and the relegating of the black man as, less than human. Now in addition to the neighborhood bars that were practically on every street corner then, add into the influx of, the other illicit or 'prescribed' forms of escapism from those pressures and hence, built was, the 'design' to keep a people in a suspended state of immobility, acceptance and wanting.

This was the war, that Christianity, the Moor's Science Temple and The Nation of Islam had been grooming people like, Sam for. I had been watching this program on organized crime in America, in my preparation for writing this story. Let me first say that, after watching this program, I came to the thinking that as many, many others may have had, in that, this country was in all essence, built on, and by, organized crime. However, one of the key things that were mentioned in this program that struck me as astonishing in regard to my writing this tome' about Sam Christian was, **"Control the crime in your neighborhood and you gain control of your neighborhood."**

The speaker then went on, to use as examples and mentioned how different races of people did this. He was also, very explicit in detail of the races of people, as he mentioned this.

He used as examples the Irish, the Italians, the Chinese as well as several other races. He did not mention however, as he was speaking of those other races, yep, you guessed it, the black race.

Now, in regard to the drugs i.e. (heroin, cocaine, as well as, marijuana, alcohol and the lot) although their grasps extended far and well across racial divides, the vast amount or epicenter where most of it wound up or, was inserted, distributed or planted, was in yep, you guessed it again, the communities mostly inhabited, by blacks and other people of color and lesser opportunities. This part of the practice naturally, made the accessibility to that immobility and acceptance easier, and decisiveness to change, less likely. I've once heard it said about Sam, that he once said, "Sometimes, you have to shock people into action." For this reason again, as I have stated that, it took a special breed of person or persons to, do or be, what Sam and the others like him chose to be, at and around, that time. That's why I have chosen again, to call them, 'The Black Ops' or, 'Special Forces' and or, as Sam had termed it, 'The Vanguard' of the movement.

Were the drugs going to be stopped? Did the government really, want or wanted them to be stopped so, as they have, and still do, profess that they do while, yet again, as they (the drugs) still to this day, continue to flood the streets and destroy families those, question again still, remain unanswered?

One thing, that was and remains evident though is, there was, and still remains, a large amount of monetary profit in that illegal trade.

As an outside observer, and not as a writer, this is why, as I have also relayed to Sam and we both found it jocularly ironic, when we spoke of how, when the media refers to him, they have done so calling him, 'The undisputed head of a criminal organization or enterprise specializing in extortion, murder and intimidation of parties involved in the drugs, gambling and prostitution businesses or trade sectors'.

Funny first, about that is, putting the nomenclature on these things as if, they are actually, (at times?) legit and acceptable busi- nesses. Well, on second thought, I guess it is when it comes to, the 'back door' and reptilian shenanigans of the 'legal' pharmaceutical businesses and their practices. The other funny part about this is, 'given the totality of all the variables and summation of the problems then and now', this title given to him is, summarily and essentially equal in analogy of answering the age-old riddle of what came first, 'the chicken or the egg?'

I'll leave it to you, the reader, and your own devices to determine finally and ultimately, for yourselves whether, Sam or, even others then or now, were the problem, or the result of the problem or again, 'business'.

Then, we will also have to finally, honestly and sincerely address, and ask ourselves 'who', is ultimately, and finally more culpable. One thing for certain though was, and although the methods and man- ners or reasons would become a good deal distorted, Sam and the

'Vanguard' were though again, as stated, on a 'fool's war that, had never been won, they were going to, 'take a stab' at correcting, the, 'problem'.

Promulgated too, at this point I believe, were such stories as, Sam, with newspapers in hand, 'going into the 'Crap' games.' Keeping in mind objectivity, and the statement by Justice Burton Roberts, "I'm not going to let you paint a picture of Al Capone" to, the prosecution or, "Robin Hood" to, the defense. I'm going to share one, of those many stories about, Sam although again, as will happen throughout now, his tome', it is he, Sam himself that, is the one telling, me.

Before going into that, again however, I'd like to lay a very important fact out on the table. As word of his coming, and reputation began to spread, so too, did the detractors. Then growing too, were those who thought, that they were up to the challenge that could, as well as a few others that wanted to, 'extinguish' that 'coming'. Several of the brothers had told me the story of how, Sam used to practice 'quick draw' in the mirror with his weapon. Also, as it had also been relayed to me, it paid off for him as well a time, or two because, "He was fast too! And he never missed! If you drew on him, you better hoped that, you got to yours before he got to his, because again, he never missed!"

Knowing, we had to get to this part of the subject, I had thought long and hard about a way to get into this important facet of the story. Recalling that revelation that was relayed to me, I had found it as, I asked, "Brother Beyah, can I ask you a hypothetical question?" "Yeah, go ahead."

"Alright, I'm a nice guy, and just for the sake of happenstance or, no reason at all, I come across some guys who might feel a certain disdain because of that. Now these guys again, for reasons beyond my even thinking or knowing about, just happen to be the type of guys that might on occasion or, as a matter of habit, carry some heat (heat, being, an urban term for, a gun) as again, a form of practice or again, just plain habit. I know that this is so, so just to be on the safe side, I carry some heat of my own for, protection. Now, on the off chance, I run into one of these guys on a bad day, and they are not feeling any qualms about using that piece (again, another sub-cultural term for, a gun) on this day, and especially against me, for whatever the reason they may happen to feel about or, against me. What would you say or think I should do?" Satisfied, that I had achieved the purpose that I had wanted to, in getting to this part, and smiling initially inside then outwardly, as he responded, "Then you better get to yours before, he gets to his."

I feel comfortable enough now, in stating a fact, which most people already knew or know, anyway.

Sam, also knows, that most people have already surmised, or knows this fact about him. Now, I would be doing you the reader, an injustice if I tried to eschew this fact.

Sam carried a gun. There, there it is!

It's out now. It was an inescapable part, and necessity of who, or what he was, and would become. And too, since we are at this part, it might as well be mentioned also that, he has used it when it was called for as well, a time or two.

Besides that, remember, it was a necessary part, or necessitated thing in being, 'a soldier' that he had been and, had so. **It was his 'sword', if you will.**

With that part, out of the way or, finally mentioned, I can now get back to the part of the story about Sam, and the crap games when he was firstly, or initially on his mission of changing or, setting things 'right' within Philly at that time.

Sam had, as it was important to evince to other people's convictions and constitutions relayed to me this part in his story of how, when he would go into the crap games and guys would respond at the awareness of his just entering, the establishment. Mind you, once again also, with an arm full of the 'Muhammad Speaks' newspapers in tow, with him.

Imagine, or picture the scene if, you would.

"Aww, shit, it's Sam, put your money away!" "Who?" "Sam! Sam Christian! Put your money away!"

And, being Sam upon hearing this. "Ain't no, 'Sam Christian' nothing. You all, ain't gotta put your money away. Ya'll don't gotta worry about me. I came to gamble just like everyone else."

Along with, selling his newspapers, and this, is what he had also in fact, came to do. Never once, have and nor will, you see it written that, Sam Christian was perfect and without his own flaws. However still, please keep in mind that, Sam was still, on a mission.

Now, the difference with Sam and the other gamblers were that, broke, crapped out or just plain busted and out of money, Sam's bank was never any of those things because, he was again, Sam Christian. Not negating or, with more focus of the objective in mind, Sam held a piece of knowledge that was either shared by, or that he, had acquired before, by virtue of, a power that is, outside of, 'the powers that be' or were at that time, of the 'business'. Please keep in mind while, observing these variables, the assertion made in that television program that I wrote about earlier on, 'Organized Crime' and one of the things that was stated in it, 'Control the crime in your neighborhood and you gain control of your neighborhood'.

Sam quickly came to the conclusion that, 'the powers that be' 'may' have known about the summation of the affects and effects of, 'business'. It was going to be, so, place the emphasis or focus on, 'Control'. By this point, Sam him self's reputation had, undulated to a point where, that scene has transcended to a vision such as this, as Sam has either tired of the situation or, was readying to conclude his un-announced visit at that particular crap game. "Bet $500.00!" Mind you again, at this point, it doesn't matter whether Sam can produce the money wagered or not.

Often times too, at this point, this is probably normally when or where, he doesn't have it. Whether, by design or fate, this is also where and when it was, 'Time to donate'. Now, I'd like to make something very clear as I am writing this, and please believe me when I say this. This fact has been thoroughly affirmed by many. When donations were made to Sam in the name of, and for the Nation of Islam, those donations were sent to where they were supposed to go, without folly or fail! In response to the opposition of that cause, and Sam while at those crap games, imagine if you will, the dialogue of, "What, I can't owe you? My word ain't no good?" The understanding that was truly shared in my belief, between Sam and the 'Powers that be' were, with the variable included of, the paramount understanding of demand being satisfied only, by supply.

They were that, the odds of any opposition to, against to or, to stop it, that would win out were at best, less than minuscule. This understanding, gave rise to the observation, the understanding of it, and the acceptance of the point that was made in the program where it was asserted that, 'control the crime in your community or neighborhood and thus, control your community or neighborhood.' It was this understanding and hope that, were the tools that Sam and others like him, at that time, had initially started out with to make those changes that were needed in the urban or black communities during the 'first resurrection' or, 'Awakening'.

A point that no one can deny is though is that, before Sam and the Nation of Islam, control and the simultaneous perpetuation or flourishing of these iniquities were overwhelmingly held and regulated by others that were, ethnically and physically from outside of those neighborhoods or communities. Yes, they knew 'business' would be 'business', but by enlisting and employing the tactics that they had, they were also serving notice, and presenting options.

To the purveyors of 'business' and its consumers, they were serving notice that,' if they were going to do business then, they would be expected to put back into the communities' although, many may argue that, those communities were not 'real' communities, but figments.

To the recipients, the 'businessmen' and other consumers of those 'businesses', they were presenting options that, they too, had a choice in their own fate or decisions. Those things, would no longer be held at the whim and or choices, of those outsiders or the iniquities that were prevalent from within the communities. In the truest essence of the word, they had given choice to a people that formally felt, that they had very few or, none at all in regard to choices, and options.

As to the final outcomes of Sam and his 'un-announced' visits at crap games. Despite a few exceptions where, he may have actually wound up leaving everyone in the crap game broke, as in, you can figure the means in, how that was done. Someone would usually, cover his back on any bet that he made so as to, avoid or stave off Sam from, 'winning' everyone's money in the crap game as sometimes, on a couple of occasions, would and had, been the case.

This is partially how, he had met such people as, Sonny Viner. Sonny, was one of those people who, in addition to, and correctly so, being a little shaken to the point of, being scared out of their wits and scared out of their wits to boot that although, as Sam was fond of saying, 'Wanted to Help' was really inside, fearful of any possible repercussions that may either be, terminal or at the least, one that would put them out of business permanently by this, so called, or alleged, *'Black Mafia'*. In other words, astute and physically beneficial it was that he, and others like him liked, or "Wanted to Help", on the normal and ephemeral perspective, he was what one from the urban environs, would call, 'rightfully frightfully' scared although, if you heard his answering machine, you would hear him calling himself, 'Big Boss Player' or something to that effect. In fact, on several occasions when some rouge thugs went into his place seemingly as if, they owned it, he had to call on Sam, and or, some of the people that Sam had associated with to, get his money back. It was one guy who, in particular would go into Sonny's place like not only, as if it was his, but also too, like clockwork or, a 'broken clock' that, the hands, were still going around and around on. Russell Barnes, was the name as, it had been relayed to me from one of the brothers of the 'First Resurrection'. Although deceased now, Russell used to go into Sonny's place as stated, like a, broken clock. While in there, he would then, take his hat off and lay it, and his two guns down on either, the Pin-ball machine and later, The Pac-Man machine or, the Juke-box. When he did this as, he never looked up at anyone while either, perusing through selections on the Juke-box or playing one of the machines everyone and especially, who was ever working the bar (Sonny or, one of his bartenders) knew, what it was and what they had to do. As People would pass by Russell when readying to leave, they would empty their pockets of all the monetary contents as they did so. This happened for a particularly long time, and especially at Sonny's place until, he had been bestowed with the opportunity or blessings of meeting, Sam Christian.

The bar that Sonny, and his wife, Neet owned and ran, was and is still located, right off of, 52nd and Market Street in the West section of, Philadelphia. Named after his wife, the bar is called, Neet's. In regard to his particular encounter and eventual actual befriending of Sonny, I will now relay as, I have deduced it to be, the precipitant and initial interaction of how that befriending became so.

Sonny, as it was relayed to me, was in his bar one night, and a customer for whatever the reason that had compelled him to do it, had reached across the bar in an attempt to strong-arm Sonny. Having had to have been in a predicament of having to have protected himself, Sonny then shot and killed the man. Through the street grapevine, it had become noted that, the man was supposed to have been connected to some real 'major' killers. Hearing of this, Sam then, put word out on the street that, Sonny was a very good friend of his, and that any retribution against Sonny for what he, had to do in protecting himself, would not be viewed kindly by Sam, and he would consider it just as much, an affront or form of retaliation against him, as it would be against, Sonny.

52nd Street as most people knew, was called, the 'Strip'. People like Sonny, as Sam was fond of saying, "Always wanted to help." Sonny himself, as told to me by Sam, was instrumental in helping him to gain a foot-hold in West Philly to accomplish what he then, and The Nation of Islam were setting out to do.

It was through Sonny also, where Sam, had met a number of people who by now, have been chronicled about or mentioned in various and different accounts of crime and the so called, 'Underworld' part of the 'business'. Sonny, in addition to being the owner/co-owner of Neet's was also, as it was relayed to me by Sam an, avid gambler so, it was not uncommon to find him at a, and the many, of the gambling spots that Sam may have happened into. Also, it was he, who had on, a many of those times, covered or backed one of those large bets made by Sam.

I guess it's safe to say that because of this, and other admirable reasons, an amicable relationship between the two was forged. As also relayed, Sonny would also on many occasions, while tending to his and his wife's bar, buy more than a fairly large amount of the, 'Muhammad Speaks,' newspapers from Sam and sell them himself or, make sure they were distributed throughout that area around there, on the Strip. Neet's, was one of a plethora of bars that were, in that part of the city around that time. It goes without saying too, that being the owner of a bar, Sonny also knew, most of the owners of the other bars and night clubs in that area, and throughout the city, as well.

Another famous bar in that part of the city that would play a major part in that part of the saga in regard to Sam's life was called, 'Mr. Silk's Third Base Bar and Lounge'. Mr. Silk's was located on, the Strip down about, and around, Spruce Street. Mr. Silk's was owned by a guy that used to actually sell at first, ladies stockings before parlaying his money and eventually opening up several bars in both, Philly and

Chester. His name was, Gus Lacey. It was not uncommon here, to see anyone from musical to sports stars as well as, the regular neighborhood people all dressed to the 'nines' or many of the alleged or so called, players and gangsters.

Also on the Strip, there were a massive number of eateries, fast foods as well as, steaks and hoagie 'joints' or, restaurants. For those, that may have happened to have been from outside of the Philadelphia or Southeastern Pennsylvania locale, 'Hoagies' are that area's, vernacular for what many others may call, 'Subs' or Subway sandwiches (a variety of different deli meats placed on about a 12 inch Italian roll with any combinations of lettuce, tomatoes or onions and seasonings to the consumer's likings or wishes).

All of these bars and restaurants gave that area of the city the feel of, one being, in a mini geography of Harlem or New York on any given night, and especially, on the weekends. And too, all of these places would become associated with Sam Christian and or, visa-versa. Speaking of New York, in addition to the other things that reminded one, of the feeling of, feeling like being in Harlem, one of these restaurants on 52nd in particularly, would also, play a very important role in the saga of Sam Christian. That such famous place, or 'steak' place on the Strip was called, Foo Foo's. Owned and operated by one, 'Foo- Foo'(a nickname) Regan and his wife, Carlotta, Foo Foo's was a place where, as all who had went there could recall or attest to, one could get the fattest, most succulent and juiciest cheese steak as many would also possibly argue, in the city.

Foo Foo Regan, was one of the first people that Sonny Viner had introduced Sam to. Carlotta, as Sam fondly relays to me, had given him the nickname, 'Big Daddy'. "Every time I would come around, she would say, 'Here comes Big Daddy!'" he says, with a wide smile.

Now, in addition to being a hot steak shop, Foo Foo's became known for, some other *'hot things'* as, it had later become noted by, the federal government or more chiefly, The Federal Bureau of

Investigations. There is something else that also must be noted at this point to dispel, many of those myths and rumors too, in regard to the initial connection between 'Foo- Foo' Regan and Sam Christian.

In regard to this connection, his main and initial purpose was so that he, Sam, could sell Foo Foo on the idea of being a distributer of the bean pies and carrot cakes that were baked at the bakeries that he, and Captain Rudolph Ali were in charge of.

These posts that they held, were at the behest of the minister of the Mosque. It must also be noted here that, being the salesman or marketer that he, Foo Foo Regan was also, in this capacity, he then became, one of the top salesman of the goods baked in those bakeries operated by the Nation of Islam throughout the city. This was also because of that, initial connection between his self and Sam. Now, another feeling that is evinced about that connection again, at this point, must also be brought up for thought.

That feeling or thought, is or was, that maybe, the meeting with Sam and Foo Foo may not have been so happenstance on the part of Foo Foo, in the scheme of things on, the scale of bigger things. Nor, do I think now, did or could Foo Foo have an inkling of the ability, to have an inkling of the understanding to, understand the profundity of what it was, that Sam was desiring to do or, to what extent, he was willing to go to, for the cause of it.

Now, although it is an already known fact that, New York was a major spot where the heroin epidemic was at a skyrocketed level, not lost on the public or federal government minds too, was also that Philly too, was one of the many major hot spots in the United States where it was also, remaining too, and at a sky-rocketed level, a major problem. And that was mainly in part of because, as it had also been noted, the Gambino crime family in New York and after Angelo Bruno's demise by death, the Bruno Crime family in Philly which was then ran by one, Nicodemo Scarfo.

And that too, in Philly was until as, that had also been chronicled or noted, the coming of the new so-called, 'Overlord' or 'Kingpin' of the distribution of that heroin which was in part, responsible for the, 'epi-pan-demic' and wonton destruction that was being distributed to both of those cities as well, as almost twenty-five others, from New York by the name of, Frank Matthews.

Frank and Foo Foo as it has been relayed to me by Sam, were, very good friends or associates. Frank, seeing the prospects of adding to his lucratively extravagant yet, poisonously toxic expanding business had inquired of Foo Foo about, adding Philly solidly, to those and one, of his assets and interests. Foo Foo then relayed to him, "The man that you need to see and talk to then, is," yep, again, you guessed it, "Sam Christian".

The reason why this referral had been made, was because again, as that had also begun, being rumored, alleged and circulated that Sam, was Jeremiah's 'Hatchet Man'. And of course, everyone knew of the disdain that The Nation of Islam held for the drug dealers that were ruining and destroying the urban and black neighborhoods.

Now, this is where I evince my point of like mindedness, in regard to, the United States or, Federal governments of the Sovereignty or Unions, and Sam, and their awareness and understanding of the in-ability to want to, or being able to or, having the ability to, stop the problem. So rather than, put all the useless energy into all-out com-batting a war that, was sure to be lost anyway and valuable good men with it, be it better to, lean more, or focus on, the ability to control it.

I feel it most important that, in stating this, that it should also be noted at this point, that this, in no way or stretch of the imagination, should it be held or, mistakenly construed or formulated that, drug dealing or the activities surrounded by it, were condoned by, The Nation of Islam.

For surety, that was not, has never, and would not ever be, the case there. And it is also with, and for surety that I can say too, to evince avuncular to that end, for such violations and suspected violations of those rules, it is also true that, Sam had been 'set down' or suspended a time or two, from The Nation of Islam.

In regard to Frank Matthews, Sam had agreed initially, to his proposition for a cost of about one hundred and fifty thousand a week and then promptly, turned his head the other way.

In doing this, I mean, turning his head as in, not seeing or caring about, the rouge robbers, dope fiends and killers who, at their own discretions and leisure would promptly, rob the people that Frank, and his main man, Tyrone 'Fat Ty' a.k.a 'Mr. Millionaire' Palmer had put into place whenever and where-ever they, the dope fiends, rouge robbers and killers chose to, and that seemed, or was, often.

Also, if you the reader like I did, a quick calculation of those numbers that Sam had been receiving from Frank Matthews. In my calculations as, I do not know about yours, I came up with an amount of, in about eight weeks' time that, added up to, approximately 1. 2 million dollars.

Also possibly, although I can't say for certain, but just possibly, I, like you the reader, started to wonder what Sam did, or would have been doing with that massive amount of money that was coming in on an exact and continual basis.

Now, possibly, you like myself, may know one thing and that is, the brevity or quickness and risks in the dope game. One thing that I had the benefit of, and will now share with you the reader is, the answers to that question from Sam Christian, himself.

Although many may see it as a bit of misnomer or ludicrous, but this is how Sam, and a number of the other brothers in Philadelphia leastwise, participated in the war against drugs initially, anyway.

Now, as to what Sam did with a large amount of that money he received from, Frank Matthews.

In explaining this, two more of the Sam's delineations in regard to the attributes that I have chosen, come to mind. One was that of, 'Caring', ''You cannot demonstrate it or define it unless, you show it. It's an action word." The other was, 'Determination', "your mind must be set on the goal. 'Plan your work then, work your plan.'" As a great number of the 'soon to be' brothers had been hearing about, and noticing the activities and impact of Sam and the Nation of Islam, they had at first, before the Nation had begun the active practice of 'Fishing' or recruiting in the city, sought out, or wanted to be a part of it. Like a lot of organizations including that of, the United States Armed Services, The Nation of Islam had a very stringent regiment and an even more stringent set of rules, regulations and requirements for its members.

In addition to those things, its members had a fulfillment of duties that they had to meet or, carry out. One of the regulations and requirements that they had to meet was, having and maintaining gainful legitimate employment. And, as another of the fulfillment of duty, its members were required to get out and spread the word of its leader and teacher, Elijah Muhammad. This chore was in part, and mainly accomplished by, the selling of its weekly newspapers, the 'Muhammad Speaks'.

For a lot of the brothers that joined and unknown, to the general public and many others, this chore was one that required a great deal of mental, physical and personal determination and energy.

It should also be noted at this point, as he has relayed it to me, that Sam in regard to this chore, and his father, was more than thankful beyond words, for the opportunity that his father had given when, he had gotten him the job working on the Schuylkill Expressway project.

What many people did not know was, when these brothers were out selling those papers while they were doing so, they were doing so, with a quota that had to be filled.

In addition to that, they also, had to pay for these, or those, yet 'unsold' papers in advance or, 'out of pocket'. This quota that was set, was set out of New York at Mosque No. 7 which, in addition to being located in Harlem, was the main and top mosque at that time.

This fulfillment however, posed a number of problems and hardships for a many of the brothers as many of them, began having problems meeting other obligations such as, paying rent, bills and taking care of theirs as well, as their family's needs and such. Although for other reasons, but especially for this one, Sam gives the highest praise and gratitude to then, Imam Wallace Dean Muhammad who, not only lowered, but eventually did away all-together with the quota system so that the brothers could tend to, and take care of other obligations.

As to what Sam did before that, to remedy the problem as he then stated to me, "I began making it my business to know who, the gamblers were and where, the gambling spots were."

Hence then, the reasons for his 'unannounced visits' to the gambling spots were because, he knew, he could sell his papers and pick up monetary assistance there, you know, 'to help'. He also too, started going out with the brothers to help them sell their papers. This last bit of information, I myself, remember personally as I recall seeing on some Saturday nights as a young kid when, these brothers would show up in my own little town all of a sudden in droves and seemingly, 'out of nowhere' looking reminiscent of either, a small platoon of men dressed in dark suits, or a large battalion of, Jehovah Witnesses. And when they came, very few, could or did, escape the area that they had embarked on which, was generally around the area of the neighborhood bar without either buying a paper or a promise of supporting the cause and plight of the Nation instead of, spending all their limited resources at the neighborhood bars and gambling spots. The funny thing to me was, even then, as I witnessed and watch this spectacle was, as I wondered to myself, which one of these guys was this, Sam Christian that, I had been hearing about. Yes, and I too, then, could remember how people would mention, or rather, whisper with timidity, his name and as they quickly tried to eschew, speaking it, or too much on, the subject about him or, it. And these were some so called, 'Bad' or revered people in their own rights in my little neighborhood that I am speaking about here, on this point. And also, even then, I could remember my wanting to, be revered, feared and spoken about, and just like that. Of course, when I got a little older, and found out about a number of the things that he was supposedly, or alleged and rumored to be involved in, that dream pretty much and quickly faded because I knew, beyond a shadow of a doubt and also, rather quickly that, I was not, a could not withstand the endurance to call myself, 'built like that'.

He then too also, started taking large portions of that money, which he extracted from such people as those, as well as Frank, and the other drug dealers and gambling spots, to help the brothers also, who again, were struggling to meet their other obligations both, with the papers and in their personal lives.

Call me misguided, call it hypocritical and then, show me any man or woman in this world without sin who, does not seek favor from their lords. Then, when you can't, show me one that does not seek forgiveness or favor from their lord in their words, actions, deeds or assets no matter what, their deeds are or were, that may if possible to, help and assist another if equipped with the resources or ability to do so.

'Straddling the Fence, the, 'Black Mafia' '

Now, just because it has been stated that Sam was a religious or spiritual man who had never lost, or forgotten his connection to his religion, it must also again, be reiterated that, that faith had been tested a time or two. It is also, most important to state this as, it may be also stated again throughout this story so as to, not mislead you the reader to think, that I am writing this prose to white wash or paint him as, some sort of saint or portrait of righteousness that had been unjustly, vilified in the media or public spotlight. In fact, it is now being reiterated again as it probably, will be again throughout to evince, show or remind that, it was that connection in as those, many times, when things had or, were going awry or, that he had felt, that, he himself, was straying too far from or just plain losing sight or, the vision of that connection.

Again, he did turn heavily, and relied on that connection (oft-times, when others around him in an immediate trying situation had faith, as the last thing on their minds).

Those times were also too, when, he was unsure of how he wanted, or needed to proceed in, taking on some of the tasks that maybe others or, those of faint heart, were unable or maybe un-willing to do. However, at that time in Philly, there was one thing that he, and others including, those of faint heart could agree upon. That was, that, the youth gang problem was growing out of control in Philly.

'Gang-warring', and or, its mentality had been becoming epidemically rampant amongst both the male and female youth population and it had to be addressed both, before, it spiraled irreparably beyond repair or, before the next step in the unity of a people, could be achieved.

Mentioned in my previous book entitled, Primacy about, 'what a morose and all-too common thing' it was too, for the number of funerals for the city's youth population that were going at any, and all too many, given times there. On the hills of the 'White flight', and the changes that had come as a result of, the heat of the civil rights movement there and throughout the United States, law-enforcement and the 'powers that be' it seemed most times, weren't too inclined to do anything other than, wait out the results of things as they would, violently transpire.

Then, as is still too often the case, they would then ardently, intervene with the intentions (and success) of, transporting the perpetrators off to jails or prison thus, in the process again, ruining forever, another young life and adding to the ranks of an angry population of men and women that were already there.

Charles McGregor, the actor that played 'Freddie' in the movie, 'Super Fly' and a fortunate representative of such, as the population that I am now speaking about, became a counselor to many of those youths and began speaking about the problem as he toured across country speaking in both, the junior and senior high schools.

During one of their stops in Houston Texas I believe it was, he had lamented on the severity, of the problem in Philadelphia. He had lamented how he was, astonished, shocked and saddened by, the number of youth that had been incarcerated there for homicides and assaults as the result of gang violence. Philly at that time, had been ranked number one in the country for, youth gang violence. I add this, to evince to the severity of the problem of what, the city had been suffering from and dealing with at that time. So again, let this not be mistaken, or misconstrued so as to, lessen, shirk or evade the responsibility or part that we again, as a people, play in the outcome of our own destiny and fate. I had once read a very good book entitled, ' What Color Justice' written by an author, by the name of, Andrew Baratta. In his book, Baratta, had painted a picture of this character, whose name was, Fullem.

Fullem, as painted by Baratta, was a racist police officer, who had murdered his best friend's and fellow officer's daughter and had set out to frame a black teenager who had been dating the girl, for the murder. In an attempt to polarize and sway his friends thinking to make him believe that, it was indeed, the black teen that had murdered his daughter, he was making a statement in regard to the difference between whites and blacks in America.

In his statement, he had said to his friend, "You know what a white man does when he gets a dime? He saves it and tries to get another one. You know what a nigger does when he gets one? He buys something shiny." I use the statement that, was made in Mr. Barrata's book not to sound, or appear acrid, but to shed a bit of light on gangs and a big part that I think of as, the reasoning for same or such.

Although, I can't truly find or give reasoning for racism, I'd like to offer up again, on what many psychologists say, is one, of the top reasons for prejudice, and that is, 'scarcity of resources'. Then, there is the number one component of prejudice and that is, polarization. Leaving race out of the equation for just a bit, and polarization being, 'a liked minded people or group, in favor of one view point, set of standards or conditions'. Then again, having, an opposing view-point or side on the other. Having first, a group whose conditions, will suffer or they will be unable to, benefit as a result of that opposition's position. Then both naturally, and mathematically one begins to, have the cause ingredients and reasons for the formation of a 'gang' or, gangs, per say.

"Gang', determining whether, or when, the term is negative or positive."

Now, before the negative connotation can truly be added to this term, one must consider, to what extent, or severity of the positives or negatives that either, will enjoy or bear, as a result of their viewpoint.

Once again, as in most cases regarding youth, the reasons or causes for the formation of a gang is, reactance. Reactance is to, 'respond incongruently or rebel against the established societal and or, parental rules of accepted standards agreed (A Greed) upon, or expected by that society's people as a whole.' Within the realms of psychology's normal expectations of reactance, this incongruity or rebellion is ofttimes as expected, not so harmful to, an irreparable and detrimental state as many, of those youth then according to psychology, grow out of it and become productive adults and members in society.

However, in regard to a more than vast surmountable amount of the so-called, youth in the urban and black communities or societies, one should, most imperatively, factor in several other precipitants, elements or obstacles to have a glimmer of an understanding in regard to, the problems of, or with gangs that were in Philly at that time. These obstacles however, even today, still persists in, and with many of the other cities throughout not, just the United States but the world abroad as a whole. One factor in particular, is to, calculate the number of, and for whatever the reasons as usually, that is incarceration and domestic reasons, fatherless homes. Then two, factor in the number of homes with teens and children living in them, which have been surviving in destitution or, at impoverished levels. Then, give that impoverished kid something 'shiny' or, something that makes them envision or feel temporarily like, that destitution or poverty is an illusion or that, that shiny thing has magically transformed them and their condition into something that is better or more enamoring than, it really is.

Then, one can see, how quickly and stronger (and without proper education) that hunger becomes a consistent and persistent longing for more, of that temporary escape from the reality of what really exists. Then, factor in the poor and uncaring failing school systems without proper awareness and understanding of the plights of these teens, and children. Then finally, factor in for these teens and children, the lack of outlets or resources to do or see anything else other than, the daily reminders of their existence in, and then of, the acceptance of that existence and ultimately, the resignation in and to, those conditions.

With that knowledge, then possibly, one could have, a workable understanding and or, some possible thoughts on a solution to the problems of 'gangs' in America and throughout the world. I do not believe that anyone could, or would have at that time, argued or, would have attributed it to luck, happenstance or fortune for, The Nation of Islam to have been the ones, in the right position or the right ones in time, to have taken on this chore.

I stand by this thought because, it was from just such conditions where, a vast number of its members came from. However, I would argue or offer as my contention to state that, it was at first, fortunate for Mosque Number 12 or, 'The Top of the Clock' in Philly at that time, that they had the benefit of one, Sam Christian and his earnest devotion to the mission and cause of The Nation of Islam. Also fortunate for, 'The Top of the Clock' was his awareness, of the aura that enshrouded, or overtook the public from the mentioning of his very name. And although he has professed to the desire of wanting to be, 'nothing more than a soldier' most importantly, to the mission was, a lesson or an awareness that he had possibly and more than likely, first realized while at, White Hill. That was in his ability to, 'polarize' and gather together the troops, or masses to assist him in any cause or endeavor that he had sought out, to achieve.

To achieve this important endeavor, it was with little to no persuasion at all, that he had amassed the best of help from all around the city. Many of these soldiers, and men, he had met and kept in his close circle also, had dated back to the time when both, he and they were at, White Hill.

There was one very deep, and common thread or piece of information that all of these men and many others whom, had encountered Sam share and hold sacred in their hearts that keeps them willingly, loyal to him despite, all that has been alleged about him or, that he has actually in fact, done. I think, that it can be stated best if, I paraphrase it as, I have heard it from one of those parties expressing that loyalty and love for him. ***"Now, Sam was no angel, but then again, none of us are.*** But, as anyone that knows him can tell you, deep down inside, you're not going to find too many people out here, with a bigger heart than, his.

A lot of that stuff that happened, those people that were doing that, were just using, Sam's name or associating themselves with his name. That's how people started putting all that stuff to his name and saying, ***'Sam Christian this,'*** or, ***'Sam Christian did that'*** and Sam, he ain't ever said nothing.

He knew they were full of shit. He wasn't even worried about it because, everybody was going to say it was him anyway. ***But deep down, Sam had a good heart and he always had that heart right through Christianity, Islam and everything."*** In regard to his, and their helping, that being, the 'Fishers of men' and the duty that they had set out upon was, to stop the youth gang violence and 'gang war-ring' in, Philly. In regard to, or in the midst doing this, there was this little piece of information of something that he had done then which, Donny Day had relayed to me that, gave me my most profound indica-tion of how strong, and serious this man was, when it came to, taking on this task.

They had been in an area somewhere around 17th and Columbia Avenue, and some guys after noticing the way that he was dressed, had asked Sam about what part of the city that he was from. Sam then verbally, served noticed, of the beginning of their mission, and his seriousness to see it through in, the cold, hard and serious stare that again, left no reason for further questioning or opposition that, he had given back to the guy when he responded, "Ain't no more North Philadelphia and South Philadelphia. It's all just Philadelphia from now on!"

Thus, and so it was too, after that.

Although ultimately, the help would come from a great number of others who, would also soon, see the imperativeness and advantages of doing so, initially, there were only a core number from with-in his inner-circle from different parts of the city there, when he first had begun. In North Philly, in addition to, Donny of course, there were a few guys that went by the names and likes of say, Georgie Benton and, Reggie Cole. If you can recall such pugilists as, Pernell (Sweet Pea) Whitaker, Meldrick Taylor, 'Machine Gun' Mike McCallum or Evander Holyfield then, you possibly and probably, may know some-thing of, Georgie Benton. Now, if those names don't and, pardon the pun, 'ring a bell' in regard to who Georgie Benton was, then maybe, you can recall, the gentleman that was in the corner of 'Smoking' Joe Frazier for his third, of three very hard fought wars against the champ himself, Muhammad Ali that took place, in Manilla. A pretty good, and very reputable fighter himself, Georgie fought his first professional

bout at the ripe old age of sixteen. He then went on to box profession-
ally from 1949 until 1970. During that time, he defeated handily such
future champs and figures, in the likes of, Joey Giardello, Freddie
Little and Jimmy Ellis. Having never been knocked down in the ring,
Georgie Benton had a professional record of 62 wins with 13 losses
and 1 draw capturing 37 knock-outs along the way.

He probably, would have still been fighting after 1970, had it not
been for, a bullet that he caught in his back by a shooter that was vow-
ing to kill anyone from the Benton clan after one of Georgie's brothers
had earlier, beaten the shooter up for having, had harassed Georgie's
sister in a bar. Georgie did not die as a result of, that bullet. He then
went on after that, with Lou Duva who had first, cheated him out of
his title shot earlier in his career, in the Giardello fight to become a
trainer for, those hosts of fighters mentioned earlier. Now Reggie Cole
who in addition to earlier, according to Sam, was first from both, the
Exiles and the Pandoras (a couple of the gangs that were out from up
in the North Philly area or section) was so sharp with his street game,
and especially cards, that, he could make it seem that he was all but,
'trimming the pockets' out of a great plenty, of the many adversaries
or opponents that he encountered whether, it was in fighting or, but
especially in, when he was playing them in, a game of cards.

Again, as it was from these men, and others, many of whom,
whose friendships he had forged while in White Hill and naturally,
well into this day, that Sam, had gotten his foot-hold and began pro-
mulgating the message and framework of their mission in a place
where, a majority of some of the roughest gangs that ever walked the
streets of Philadelphia, were situated. Here, in this part of the city
with such gangs as, the **Exiles**, the **Morrocos**, the **Tenderloins** and
the **'Valley'** most, fell right into line without problems or rebuttal to
the call of, stopping the gang warring. Donny, his life-long friend, as
we have made note about previously, was, from the Valley up there in
North Philly also.

Of course, as most people who were raised up in that part of town and around that time knew, the *Valley*, was probably, the largest of all of those gangs up there, in North Philly. Having that advantage, and Donny Day on his team, can probably evince as to why, Sam did not encounter much resistance from too many, of the other gangs up there.

Now, this was not to say that Sam did not encounter any problems while he was setting out on his mission because, as we have also stated earlier, although on a mission and new awakening, he was still straddling a fence. That was a little bit after, and how, and when, he had encountered a certain woman who, would become although neither of them knew it at that time, the mother of two of his daughters.

This woman had a brother. His name was Sauladeen. Like Donny Day, Sauladeen was also, from the Valley gang up in North Philly. Unlike, Donny Day though, Sauladeen at first, wasn't too keen on coming along with Sam when, he had first set out on his, mission of changing things, in the City of Brotherly Love.

And that, wasn't due to the fact that, Sam was involved with his sister either, that Sauladeen at first, wasn't open to this idea. In fact, the revelation of Sam's involvement with Sauladeen's sister was a revelation that came about in the damndest way and also, may have (somewhere in time, spirit and space) been the reason why, Sauladeen may have eventually opened up, and came along in the end. You see, the reason why Sauladeen was not initially open for the idea of Sam being the guy that would be the precipitant or figure-head of the what, that they were attempting to accomplish was because, like Sam was to, and in South Philly, Sauladeen was and or is, to North Philly through and through. Also, in addition to the Valley Gang being, one of the largest gangs in North Philly, they were also probably, one of the biggest gangs in Philadelphia. So, it was for that reason and that reason only, that Sauladeen, wasn't big on the idea of Sam being the figure-head or the one, to be alluded or referred to when, they were setting out on their mission.

And, Sauladeen had no qualms in his willingness to prove, or evince that point, either. Nor, was Sam any less firm in his convictions either, to say, the least.

As it turned out, one night up in North Philly, and in, what was, the Valley turf no less, things came to a head.

That was when, after some heated words, Sam, had commenced to, firing on Sauladeen and some of his 'crew' or 'people' who were, or just happened to have been other members of the *Valley* gang. After dispersing, Sauladeen, and a few of his crew, came back to the building where, Sam and a few of his people (actually, just Donny) had retreated up to the second flight of. In the ensuing blaze of gun-fire that then took place, both, Sam and Sauladeen were ultimately hit, by bullets.

When the bullets were flying, they weren't firing as to scare, or as to fire any, warning shots either. They were firing for intent and deadly purpose. Hit by one of the slugs and hanging on the precipice of passing out as, he was coming down the stairs with his guns still blazing, Sam then surely on that night, and for one of the rare few times, was thankful that the shooters had heard the sounds of the on-coming police sirens and had decided to back off and again disperse.

Sauladeen now, was not only a part of probably, the largest gang in the City of Brotherly Love and was to, North Philly what Sam was to South Philly, but he was also a part of, a rather large family in as far, as blood relatives went, as well.

Upon hearing of what had transpired, they had all then, converged on the hospital that both he, and Sam were transported to with he, on one floor and Sam on the other. Determined to see who this other guy was who, had attempted to take his son's life and more determined, to make sure that he would never get another opportunity to do so, Sauladeen's father and a couple of others went down to the room that Sam was being treated in. Upon getting there, it was then that Sauladeen's father was faced with a conundrum that could have almost been as equaled to that, of none other than, King Solomon or, Sulieman, himself.

It was and while there, that the revelation had been revealed that, his daughter and, Sauladeen's sister had been involved with the shooter whom of course, as we already know, was none other than, Sam himself. Suffice it to say that, after witnessing this, that all of the differences between Sauladeen and Sam were quashed for surety, certainty and forever.

Sauladeen and the rest of the *Valley* upon that revelation, then came along, or in, with Sam and the cause after that. With the support and backing of the *Valley* along, the rest of North Philly easily without any duress or coercion, smoothly followed suit. Now, this again, is not to say that there were not any other gangs in North Philly that could not contend or stand up to, the challenge should, they have chosen to. No, by no means, let this be construed as, the case. There were several others up there that could, if they had so chose to. Namely one was, the Tenderloins. They had in their crew a guy by the name of, 'Nudie' Mims. By now, you've not only read in here about the pedigree of Nudie but also, as you may have heard in all the other stories of the alleged, *'Black Mafia'* of, some of the things associated with his name, as well. There in North Philly, were a great number of others, which were cut from the same cloth as, Sauladeen and Nudie. Before I move on from North Philly, I must add one other name and him into, or onto, that list.

Should you perchance, happen to venture in and through certain parts up there, mention and see does the name, Grady Dykes also, and again, pardon the pun, 'ring a bell' or two, in a great many minds, there too? In fact, in case I failed to mention or, I had glanced over, it was he that, was the one, who had, peppered Donny's chest and Donny into temporary submission causing, Sam to want to cut in for him, Donny at White Hill thus causing, the whole facility then, to go into 'lock-down' mode.

For the now, and present though, in regard, and on the note of Sam and Sauladeen's relationship.

In addition to Sauladeen eventually coming along, and assisting Sam in what it was, that they were setting out to do with the Nation of Islam and the gang situation, although his relationship with Sauladeen's sister may have taken the course that it did in as, Sam and she parting ways, his relationship with Sauladeen became one that, had become endeared and as thick as those, of even, Sauladeen's own natural blood brothers and sisters that has lasted well into even, this very day.

To evince to the extent of the bond of that relationship, it was a thing worthy of awe to see how, people transformed and shuddered when it was, or had been found that, Sauladeen, had received word that someone mayhap, had the thought of transgressing against, or had offended Sam in any way.

In West Philly, he had relied also, on his alliance with, some heavy weights that he had attended Boone with by the names of, Al Creighton and Harold 'Piggy' Frambo. Al Creighton who, in addition to being, a pretty well-known and highly respected individual throughout West Philly amongst the well represented hosts of others gangs that were there, was the main one that, Sam alludes to when he speaks of learning, how to box.

'Piggy' or, Brother Nasir as those, within the, 'Brotherhood' or ranks referred to him as, in addition to becoming, a close friend and inspiration to my own self, was known for, being pretty much, hell, damn good with his hands as, well.

In fact, he was so good that, living and coming up in the part of the city that he did, (The Black Bottom) which, was separated from North Philly only by, the literal, Philadelphia Zoo, guys from North Philly and other parts of the city thought long and hard because, they pretty much guessed correctly, that it was going to be no easy 'chore' when one, went down there in Piggy's office or, part of the city, to mix things up with him and his boys, there.

Finally, to round things up, or to, put the finishing touches to his tapestry of the perfectly formed and able-bodied subjects to help him to achieve his objective, he then, went deep into the trenches of West Philly up around, the 54th and Ludlow and the Walnut Street areas.

There, he enlisted the assistance of a couple of real 'sharp' West Philly street savvy individuals who, used to be from one of the gangs up there called the, **Barbary Coast,**. John Pickens or, Brother 'Yah Yah' as he was known, amongst and in, the brotherhood services would be to, with both the 'fish' and newly minted brothers within the Nation of Islam, go around to all parts of the city to keep fresh in the minds of the former gang members the message and objective that they were seeking to spread and achieve. In addition to this, his other job was also, to garner support for the 'Top of the clock'. The objective and message was simple and, just simply stated, that one objective and one message. The objective was to, give the people a knowledge of themselves and their possibilities of being or, doing something more meaningful and positive other than that, which they had been doing, or were presently, accepting.

The message was this, 'Violence begets violence and that violence is not conducive to, and nor, is it productive to achieve that objective of knowledge of self and possibilities. Rather, it is a hindrance and inhibitor of that objective. So, henceforth, anymore of the senseless killing of the youth as the result of, gang violence or by, the so called gangs, would be addressed by a group with a cause, a great deal larger and stronger than any of the gangs combined.'

And that retribution for that violence, would be met with, and as equal to, or more severe chastisement in turn for the transgression. Although one could conclude that, that meant, the Nation of Islam.

However in larger part, it meant not a 'gang', but a group of like-minded individuals in, and for the greater cause of righteousness. Needless to say, but it must be mentioned that, Sam's support in their cause in South Philly was melded a long time before any of this, which was conceived or transpired as there, ever present were, Kenyattah (Spooks) Bey and his wife, Alma.

After having had first also, attended Boone with him and then becoming, a lieutenant and staunch supporter under his, Sam's command in the Nation of Islam, Brother Sultan Shabazz (Tyrone Irons) who was often called upon when it came to, educating and articulating to the public as well as those, in public office outside of, 'The Top of the Clock' about the Nation of Islam and its goals then, became one of Sam's most trusted spiritual advisors to complete his initial roster of 'help'.

One other thing, which must be noted here. In regard to these men, when I say, or use the term here, 'Help', I mean that in the most ardent and equal terms of respect and brotherhood that these particular individuals had, give, and gave to each other. This was a far cry from which, I use the term in regard to the others or, 'outsiders' that I had or might, mention.

I must admit that, there was a point in my life when I had become disillusioned and exasperated with the whole Christianity concept and the 'Jesus' thing. "Fishers of men. It's in the Bible. Peter was an intercessor for man. 'I will make you my disciples, 'fishers of men'." is what Sam, had said to me, when we had first began discussing this chapter. Exasperated or not, there was one character in the Bible that, I had kept in my mind, and could easily recall as, I would go through certain situations in my life.

That character was the one named, Judas Iscariot. In regard to Sam, and those like-minded others, who had gathered together to be 'Fishers of men', amongst them also too, was an individual whose character became (in the public's eye and mind) likened to that of, that character in that Bible that I had just mentioned, by name of, Judas Iscariot in that same, Bible.

Likened to that character in the Bible, who had sold his friend, Jesus to the Romans for a pocket full of Six Pence, he too (in that same public light), would be perceived to be the one that would, sell his own brothers out and all that they had sought to achieve to the will and desires of the devil for his own, selfish desires and greed or, so it to many, would seem.

Now the dichotomy of that individual was that, as adamantly as I, you or anyone else may feel and commiserate about him or, and at that particular point, I must also adamantly stand firm in my conviction and staunch belief in saying that, when he had first came into the awakening or light of what it was that he, and the brothers were attempting to do, there was no one more committed and with more conviction than he either.

Another point in regard to, that same individual, that must also, be mentioned in this pertaining to, Judas Iscariot, when he committed the transgression and betrayal that he had against Jesus, he found little if any at all, except for, his creator that, would show forgiveness never mind, the understanding of his sin.

In regard to this, or, that commonly perceived modern-day Judas that would seemingly, and ultimately, betray his brothers and the charge that had been given to him with The Nation of Islam.

Unlike the Judas Iscariot of Christ times, he would however, find many that, would and willingly did, follow him down that path of iniquity of their own volition. I add this again not, to cast aspersions on him, or any of the others, but to further show proof, or evince that despite the greatest of intentions, how easily that it is, for that intent, to be dissuaded by the enamoring and seemingly glorified tools that ultimately caused and will again, be the cause of many, of our demises, those being, vanity and possessions. Also again now as, I inject this point or observation not to, validate, glorify or justify any of the things that Sam has, was alleged to have had or, had been rumored or actually, had done. However, I do offer it up again now, to show or evince to, his strength in his conviction of fortitude.

Reiterating again on how, it has been said about Sam, and his contentions that, "I never wanted to be anything but a soldier" in this regard in his life where, that conviction was tested to the upper and uttered most extreme, and has been proven affirmed to an even, more so over of, one.

This was when, as it had been relayed to me, from a very reliable source in this regard that he had been once overheard, to have said on one occasion, to a certain or, deceiver of whom he had, with all of his spiritual fortitude, supported and trusted, " You better not ever lose that position! Hold on to that position! Because, if you ever lose it, I'm going to kill you."

And despite all that, and what had transpired, Sam held true, in regard to his betrayer, and his avowal and allegiance to that which, he had sworn to hold allegiance to as, he respected and stood true to his betrayer, and for a long period after that particular, and egregious transgression or betrayal, afterwards.

But, of things that, we can't explain, that turned out in a sense of evenness that, we can't explain either. Inebriated by, and of, the drunken and delusional scent of power or the perception of it, by the party, and what it caused them to commit again, that most egregious transgression is what had caused Sam to have made that, 'more serious and meant to be taken adherence to', statement.

Now, 'The Top of the Clock' mosque, did not always have the luxury of being situated at its structure of where it was located at in Philly as when, they had started out, they had to set up gatherings and meetings in such places as, meeting halls and in, people's homes. In this regard, this is where Sam and others, as again, it had been relayed and from again, another very reliable source, were thankful for the services, assistance, perseverance, fortitude, determination and dedication to service of one, John Clarke.

Like, Sam himself, John Clarke was known through-out the ranks as either, Brother John 38 or simply, the, 'Rock'. John Clarke was, as were they all, a staunch believer, and supporter of the Honorable Elijah

Muhammad. He was also, a pinnacle reason why, and how, a great number of those house meetings for a large number of perspective as well as, members, in the Nation of Islam before the mosque was built, took place.

He was also, ardently successful and adamantly instrumental in, garnering donations for The Nation of Islam. And like Sam, if 38, had set out to make a donation to the minister and Nation and was successful, the donations made it to where, they were supposed to make it to. For a great proportional number of disbelievers and violators also, against the honorable Elijah Muhammad, the name and person of 38 was again also, something else to be, dreadfully feared as well, when it came in the presence of, and for that cause, and of the, 'Rock'.

If Brother Sultan was one of the finishing touches in regard to Sam's spiritual adviser or advisory, then, the 'Rock' was truly, his mortar in the finishing touches on his physical conviction, fortitude of, and on, the cause. In the spirit of integrity and as promised, the truth, that in writing this, I am bound and beholden by. And by being so, I am also, bound and compelled to elaborate on the 'Rock', and a minute portion of some of the things and events associated with his name for those, that may not as of this writer's writing, know of, or who, the 'Rock' was and how profound of a part that, he played.

Again, and as the result of research and by both, a reliable and close source and the accounts of public news records and sources in events surrounding John 38, 'While on bail for a totally complete different case, a couple murders in Philadelphia, he was then arrested for the kidnapping of a bank manager and his family with the purpose of, taking him to the bank the next morning to clean out the vault. Scared beyond his wits, the bank manager jumped out of the plate glass window. And subsequently 38, and several of his accomplices were arrested. While in custody at, Lewisburg Federal Penitentiary, 38 was then indicted as one of the accomplices in, the Hanafi murders in Washington D.C.

However, 38 never made it to trial for any of those, crimes. After securing power in Lewisburg Prison which, was predominately ran by other different prison gangs, 38 supposedly, or allegedly, died of a heart attack. This 'supposed' heart attack was also, the end result of several other of the prisoners who were connected to either, the Nation of Islam or the Hanafi murders as well, at that time.

Of the Hanafi murders, we will again as promised, elaborate and expound on it, a little bit more and, a bit later. Word was circulated in the prison that 38's heart attack was the result of being poisoned 'while in custody.' And it was with that roster, that Sam and the others, had set out to make the changes that they thought would be advantageous for the people as a people, and as, whole in the city. Sam was one time also, to have been over-heard, and was said to, have stated again that, "Sometimes you have to shock the people into thinking". As many may agree, the government used to, and still does do it, all the time. And as, if one falls into that realm, and may agree, 'now, the poison is given on such a liberal and consistent basis or degree that, it could be considered quite a task to, actually now days, 'Shock' many into sincere and critical thinking.'

I had inquired of Sam in regard to his concurrence or, of his, having knowledge of making that statement. He affirmed to the positive on both accounts in regard to that particular, query.

"I know what's on your mind. You really want to know, don't you? I mean, it's actually eating you up inside to know isn't it? Listen Brother, we loved Malcom! Malcom was a true, and beloved brother that we loved, like our own flesh and blood-brothers. We would have followed Malcom into war and would have, died for, him. It was just that, we loved our leader, (The Lamb) and our spiritual teacher, the Honorable Elijah Muhammad more. Although we were different men then, and that was where our situation and belief systems had been steered or geared towards, our thinking was, we couldn't have the presence of Malcom and the direction or position that he had chosen for himself, eclipsing that of, our beloved leader and teacher."

There was no F.B.I cover-up or any, of the other far-fetched, hair-brained theories that had been, hashed and hatched thus far. It was simply for that, and that reason only. There was no scheme or plan hatched by The Nation of Islam or any other governmental agency to assassinate Malcom.

"It was that which, was our sincere devotion to our spiritual leader that, I was compelled to do what, I had done."

And with that, the speaker then stated to his inquisitor and listener, "And with that, I'm going to turn over and go to sleep." This conversation that took place may have the ability, and may very well, shock a few individuals. But in addition to, and with, that shock value to the side for a moment, it was again at this time resonated, to evince to, the power of, 'conviction' and of such men's, sincere and uncompromising devotion to, it.

So there, is the unequivocal, unadulterated and objective truth in regard to, Malcom X. He was not assassinated by or, for his beliefs nor later, lack thereof, in the Nation of Islam or its, leader.

But rather, and once again unequivocally, unadulterated and objectively, he was murdered by one for his, particular beliefs in the Nation of Islam and its leader. Although we will expound further in Sam's story about his relationship with another person of whom, had played or rather, made a very important and valuable impact into Sam's life, I want to expound or highlight on, a conversation that he, that individual had with another individual with whom, Sam was also closely, connected and associated with, and with it, regard to conviction.

All the first individual inquired of the second one was, "Did you do it?" When the second individual responded, "Yes.", all that the first individual responded with was, "Then, you have to turn yourself in." With that, the second individual then promptly turned themselves over or into the authorities.

That conversation that took place was between, Robert 'Nudie' Mims and another very important individual that would play an, and the most profound part in regard to Sam Christian, and the power of his conviction, acceptance of it as well as, his ultimate conciliation with it within his own, self.

The conversation that took place, was in regard to an incident that took place on, January 4th, 1971 at then, Dubrow's furniture store on, South Street. Convictions? A number of reasons both, plausible and not so palpable have been given as the catalyst for what, had transpired on that day. Now, I have it on, and from, a reliable source that, the main catalyst whether plausible or not so palpable was, for a conviction much deeper than those charged by law-enforcement and the outside observer, in general.

Although it may be viewed as a small diminutive thing given the gravity, and in light of, the incident that took place at Dubrows, still, to many especially, in the urban community of Philadelphia, it was one that had played both, a major and crippling to, any ideas that one on either side, could use as a continuance of their and, un-just, lowly conditions, behaviors and or existences. This was when the stories such as say, the likes of a Dubrow's and crippling part to any ideas that one may have had, of moving or advancing ahead let alone, in addition to, their just everyday consistent maintenance of their lowly paid and 'un' or under-appreciated existences.

This was when stores such as say, the likes of a, Dubrow's was in the practice of, their own form of 'predatory' lending. It might quite possibly be true, that many these days, may have perchance forgotten about when such stores again, like that of, Dubrow's used to offer, or lure people into buying that on-the-surface extravagant furniture and or, other house-hold items that, they used to sell.

Also too, many may have forgotten about those astronomically and exorbitantly high interest rates that, those stores again, like Dubrow's used to charge people at least, in the urban community for, the opportunity to purchase on credit those again, on-the-surface extravagant items that one could once upon a time, purchase at only, such places as, Dubrow's and the, likes.

However still as it was, a great number of those people did, do business with Dubrow's and like, other stores. And although not too many of them would admit it now, they did also, do business with the likes of Dubrow's and other like stores in also, just such a manner as that, described.

Because of this, Dubrow's and once again, those other like stores, held a lot of those people whom, may have forgot as, economically 'bound' hostages. This fact, was evinced in the books and records that stores like those, of say, a Dubrow's or the others kept. Before computers, and the other technological advancements and developments, many who choose to remember, may possibly remember how, those annoying and incessant collectors would knock on doors, or call, and harass all hours of the day and night, the now bounded prisoners who, had been persuaded or manipulated into buying those, on-the-surface house-hold items and other things from such stores as, Dubrow's and the likes that, before long, didn't seem so enamoring and enticing.

And nor now, would many of them, want or want you to recall how, jubilated, vindicated and just plain freed many of them felt, when they had found that, many of their sentences (bills), had been pardoned or exonerated in the burnt out offices of Dubrow's that day save, although, there were many.

Again, and although I am neither, condoning or can be considered as one to, condemn Jahbar's or 'Nudie's' actions for, it is not my place to, I'm just further evincing my point on convictions, and further to, impose the question of people's willingness or extent that they would go to, in defense of it. Keeping in mind Sam's assertion that, "That's what it was, it was a war." one could, make the most assured assessment or assertion that, although in the eyes of a conflict, the matter of either terrorist or, patriot is of the opinion of either, the advocate of or, of that opposed, to a position on that day, a great blow was delivered that liberated and freed up a great number of people in favor of the position on the side of what Jahbar did. And that again, was in spite of what others of an opposing view point, may hold, have held or, would have concede to, although again, not many of either viewpoint would verbally concur to.

There was another thing that came out of the incident, which took place on that day. That was when all of a sudden, you didn't have anywhere, those incessant vampires of that machine called, 'timed payments' so eagerly, and anxiously feeling the feeling of the unadulterated liberty and freedom to, at their leisure and whims, knock on the doors of their unsuspecting and unaware of that part of the plot, blacks, poor and other people of color and or, minorities in the City of 'Brotherly' Love or any of the other cities, alike.

These were just some of the extents, depths and willingness of conviction that many of the people that 'Samuel Richard Carter' surrounded himself with, were willing to go to, when they had embarked on their mission of changing things in the City of Brotherly Love. Again, neither condoning nor condemning, just stating.

Samuel, Richard, Christian.

With so many different paradigms or castigations in regard to the general public's opinions and perceptions of Sam Christian, like he, and as I have had the opportunity to witness, many of them, had started to sound repetitive and mundanely boring.

On this note, I can now honestly and sincerely, express my empathy in his reasoning for, when he lowers his head or looks off and away from the party that he mayhap be speaking with as if, in search of something more interesting than the inquisitor's tiresome questions. Here, I am further reminded of the time when as, he and I were sitting outside of the Sister Clara Muhammad School in Philly after a Friday Jumah prayer. Earlier, on that particular day, after the Jumah prayer, there was a misunderstanding between Donny and myself and, Donny was rather heated about it. We had exchanged some rather terse, but un-offending words. But later, after the misunderstanding or the air had been mixed up, and hashed out and then, cleared up, we had both, apologized to each other for the things that had been said.

No, that's not quite right. Donny, being the man that he was, I should say, after thinking about what had caused the misunderstanding stated, "Nah, you know what? Ever since I've known you in the short period that I've had, I've known you to be a stand-up guy. I'm not going to take the word of someone, I don't even know, over the word of my brother. I apologize." Later, while sitting outside of the school, just Sam and myself, Sam had seen that although, I was quiet, my pensiveness had shown that, I was still a little bothered by, what had transpired between Donny and myself.

Without a word from me, he then looked off and away as if, he were, thinking about or, reflecting on some other thoughts himself that, were of much more importance than, what had transpired between Donny and myself (and again, he was right). Then, with a tired, dismissive, consoling and lazily seeming, 'shooing away' wave of his hand, he says to me, "Don't let what Donny said, get to you. I just put Donny on my, 'Pay him no mind' list sometimes." It was with his next statement, that it had really been confirmed that, he was indeed, thinking, or reflecting on something more, and really deeper, profoundly.

It had shown me how alone, mind you, alone not, 'lonely' that he, had felt. Not just then, but throughout his life. It had shown me how much he knew that, time had passed or moved on.

It had opened my eyes up further, as I watched and took in how, the many around or, of those wanting to be around him, that flock to him wherever, he may go, that for whatever the reason, didn't seem to realize that. I guess that too, was, that thing which, I had wrote about earlier in that seeming, state of being awe-struck or the, 'deer in the headlights' thing. It had reminded me, of just how, 'sharp' and attuned that he had been, and still was. It had also further, re-iterated to me of just how much, at peace he was, within himself.

With just him and I, and nobody else around on that day, with the ground still speckled with the brown and gold leaves and the season on the cusp of turning into spring, on the stoop directly, outside of the Sister Clara Muhammad School tired, resignedly and seemingly bored he then says to me, "These guys are just sitting around waiting for Superman to come back and, he ain't coming back." By 'these guys', he had meant, not just a great number of the brothers in the masjid, but also too, the flocks of people that know, may think they know or those, that may have heard about, Sam Christian.

Now, in the spirit of truth and honesty on another note, I had gathered from some of those same people and he, a couple of things that, I would not have imagined in a million years given, that same public's contrasting or incongruent opinion about him.

There was for instance, can you imagine Sam Christian a dancer? Now although I am not speaking about a ballet, tap or any sort of stage dancer, I am according to, some of his close associates talking about, a pretty good dancer. Thinking of Sam Christian, the 'gangster', I had to laugh as, it was relayed to me that, "Yeah, Sam used to dance his butt off." "Sam?" I asked, sincerely amused, finding it hard to coincide the persona and this revelation. "Yeah, he would be up in the parties doing the Cha-Cha and the split and everything." Then thinking again about his family roots and he, being grounded in the church as, I recalled him telling me of how, he, his mother and his sisters Coretta and Sandra made up the church group in their church called, 'The Family Four', I guess that, it wasn't too hard to imagine of where, he had gotten his rhythmic ear and coinciding talents of expression in the form of dance to later secularize, or make the short transition to that of, the dance floor or 'blue light' parties and such. This particular talent or revelation may have also, lent credence to, another.

That was, of how Sam too, became known as quite a womanizer, as well. I guess one, can't really blame that last one all on Sam seeing in as how, a lot of woman had and still have, that seemingly biological and carnal desire to have themselves attached in some way or another to, that image of the, 'bad boy' or 'tough guy' figure.

One thing that can't be denied, negated or minimized in expounding on, in that last part in regard to, Sam the dancer though. And that is, one could almost with surety and certainty, state that this, the womanizer part may have again with surety and certainty, played a major role in him becoming a father to the vast number of children that he eventually had as again, that number last tallied, totaled, past twenty.

Jeremiah Shabazz, the genius Judas that, could have been like, Jesus.

In addition to, and before in 1960 for, being responsible for bringing the Champ, Muhammad Ali into the folds, and ranks of the Nation of Islam, and becoming, the minister of, 'The Top of the Clock' Jeremiah, had been bread in and not only survived but, eventually went deep forth within, and was bringing forth to see, for the America at that time without, the benefit of rose-colored glasses or sugar, the hypocritical, colonialist and horrendous atrocities that she, Lady Liberty herself, was committing against not only the true natives or inhabitants of a country that she herself had also, robbed, raped and pillaged but of, the other peoples of other continents and coast the she had also, connived and then robbed, as well.

And keeping things now, in the context of what Sam had stated to me earlier in his saying, 'That's what it was, it was a war!' towards none, and no place else was this more evident than, to a people or race than in, at that time, one of African descent or, the 'black man' in America. Such an ardent, fiery and fervent spirit and force for the Honorable Elijah and the Nation of Islam was Jeremiah at first, as it has been relayed to me, that he once, on his own and by himself, walked into a Ku Klux Klan meeting and exclaimed to all of them that were present, that they were the 'devils' and the devil's incarnates themselves.

Born in Philadelphia Pennsylvania in 1927, after first graduating from Benjamin Franklin high school, and then serving, in the United States Army in, the United States Signal Corps at the conclusion of World War II, he first began working for the United States Postal Service in the capacity as, a civilian employee.

Joining the Nation of Islam at a very early age, he then in 1954, began working with Malcom X Shabazz, in his native home town of Philadelphia to establish his faith, and religion amongst the people there. Around 1958 or 1959, he was then, at the behest and orders of Elijah Muhammad, sent down first to, Atlanta to spread the message of the 'Lamb' to, the people there. After arriving there, he then went on to, help establish places (houses) of worship throughout the states of Georgia, Florida, Mississippi, Louisiana, Alabama and Texas as well as, other places throughout the Southern sections of the United States. After returning back to Philadelphia as the minister of Mosque number 12 or, 'The Top of the Clock' he then, built up its membership to approximately, six thousand strong as more began joining, each day. Building bakeries and stores throughout Philadelphia, 'The Top of The Clock' had then, become known as one, of the top mosques throughout the Continental United States.

'If a sinner attends a church, does that make the church a bad place?' I am fully aware of the label that was placed on Mosque number 12 also, at the height, of everything that had transpired. However, as it had been stated in one of those documentaries by later, police commissioner of the Philadelphia police department, but then around that time, police officer, Willie Williams, "What I saw when, I was there," in the beginning and now once again, was a place where, a great deal of those, found refuge there, found strength, thrived and went on, to do great things. I don't think there is anyone that, can refute that point.

I am also, aware of what, has been stated in regard to, the number of so-called, 'criminal element' that would eventually, wound up in its ranks. However again, I ask the question that,' *if a sinner attends a church, does it make the church a bad place?'*

Please keep in mind that, before many of these so-called, 'criminal element' attended there, that like many people of color, opportunity for most, to be anything else other than 'criminal' in most urban neighborhoods was all but, a moot point. As it was lamented in that program, 'American Gangster', although in a different context, 'this was especially true, in Philadelphia'. As it was also expounded on in that same program that, although again, in a different context that most of those, "criminal element" that had attended there, had found a light, cause or reason what-have-you, to do, or give thought about something other than, what was there for them, in Philly for them besides, what was there for them, in Philly otherwise. Still, as I am not attempting to shun, make excuses or negate responsibility for the number of things, that had ultimately transpired, I am desiring that you, the judge by hearing this story keep in mind, a sentiment that was relayed to me by, one of those brothers and that, had also been echoed, by a number of others and that, I am now, echoing again. That was, **"We were not bad people. We were sincere people whose sincerity, was misused and abused."** Also, there are several other thoughts that I would also like, resonated in your thought process as you ponder on the degree or depths of the atrociousness that was the result of those same things that, had taken place during those events.

A few of them were for starters, that one, although the Nation of Islam in then, and its future desires were desiring to, purchase a plane for its leader, that they or the members of that, 'criminal element' in or, at the 'Top of The Clock' did not own any of the planes or ships that were used for, the transport of that scourge that ultimately caused, what happened, to transpire. Then there was, in comparison, if one wants to really lay blame and lament what a horrible person that Jeremiah was, and as barbaric and reprehensible the things that, 'criminal element' and he, had made and caused to transpire, they would have to take into consideration a number of other things or events that had taken place over the course of history and then, and only then first, and honestly, address them and decide whether, they are truly ready, to be addressed and or, if those that committed those atrocities, are truly ready, to make amends for them.

Like for instance, is America truly ready, to accept responsibility for such conflicts as, 'The Vietnam conflict or, 'Police action' where, in addition to the 58,209 deaths that occurred as a result of that action, the number of total dead and wounded added up to 211,454 not to say, anything of the still now, lingering problem of the remnants that were sent home from there addicted to drugs and alcohol and the post-traumatic stress disorders caused by it. Then, there is the results of the Gulf war conflict that, is responsible for the deaths of another 1,143 American lives. In addition to that, are we really ready to deal with the 20,904 lives that were lost as a result of, the Afghanistan conflict and let alone, the scores of those veterans, that are still struggling to reconcile, their lives that were turned upside down and disseminated because of it. Then, there is still, the so-called, 'Iraq conflict'.

A covert operation, which was disguised as a conflict to liberate, and free the lives of the people of that country and to search for, 'Weapons of Mass Destruction'. When in reality, all who know any little tad-bit of information about that 'war' knew, that it was nothing but, a sham to further, line the pockets of the greedy 'Big Wigs' and so called, 'Oil Barons' that thought in addition to, pulling a sham over the public's eye, that they would also gain control of, that country's oil fields and other resources. Finally, in regard to the numbers, casualties and lives destroyed, we must also, be ready to confront this so called, 'War on Terrorism' where, that total, all tallied caused, the lives of 57,614 combined between the, Afghanistan and Iraq conflicts.

Now, to the problems of drugs and the resultant problems caused by it, in America. Before we really go deep into casting aspersions on the so-called 'Pushers and drug dealers' and 'criminal element' in this country, in addition to, not one of them or, anyone of in-opulence owning any planes to transport that scourge that has disseminated many lives of people not only in America, but throughout the world, we must first honestly and realistically, deal with some other aspects in that regard. This reminds me, of this 'me-me' that I recently read, on one of those social networks that read, 'If, we lie to the government it's called, a crime, but if they lie to us, it's called, politics'. This in turn, reminds me of something else that had once came into my mind, and how, I formulated it my mind, as a play on words and what, I had come up with as the end resultant and, that was the word, 'Politics'. I had separated the word, and had come up with the following, 'Poli' and 'tics'. The word, 'Poly' or, 'Poli' as you know how the 'i' and 'y' are sometimes, in the English translation inter-changeable where they both at times, can form the long 'e' sound is, of Greek origin. Akin to the old English translation of, 'Fela', 'Fellows' it means, 'Many'. And well, the word, 'tic', 'tick' or, 'tics' if you're using it to describe, plural meaning, 'more than one' you might already know where, I'm going with that in the form of, 'parasi(tic) arachnid, all *pertaining to,.

Back to my overall point here, at this juncture, in this story. And never mind for a minute when, speaking of the 'criminal element', the people like one, Carmine Tramunti that many say, was responsible for introducing, and then flooding, the streets of Harlem with that scourge that has again, destroyed many lives there. Never mind also, for a minute, people like, Vito Genovese or even, Frank Matthews.

We would first, have to honestly, go back further, like say to, 1874 Germany and then, we can begin to address the questions of, 'who' it is, that is really, at fault or, the 'criminal element' responsible, for a vast amount of the 'drug' problem that exist throughout the world today. Because it was there, where, some scientist took the opium plant and after extracting the use of the morphine in the drug, then extracted further, the problem that now largely exists, in this country today, heroin. Starting out in Philly, this is what the brothers had at first, started out to combat. True, as it may have been that, many of these brothers came from or were groomed in an environment that promulgated (Philadelphia being what it was then, with limited opportune for people of color) or led to, what has been described as, them being, of the 'criminal element', but when, they had happened upon, or had found their way or, had been led into, the Nation of Islam, many of them with great sincerity and intentions had sought, or had wanted to, leave those things and ways, behind.

For this reason, I posed the question that, *'If a sinner walks into a church, does it make the church, a bad place to go?* Again, not casting any aspersions but, if that be the case, then because of, the activities of many of the members of the so called, *'La Cosa Nostra'* or, the other alleged, *Mafia* that attended the Catholic churches, that in this writer's opinion, would be considered, hell in itself, in that same context of one's thinking.

However, and along with, the thinking of most others, as I am also forced or compelled to, 'minutely' concur with, when one in a position of leadership openly condones or encourages criminal activity or incongruent behavior of those, seeking or desiring benevolent or providential refuge or guidance, then there, with that particular party not the sanctum, should and could blame be rightfully, and justly lain.

It would also be unfair, in this writing, as it has also been stated, not to state that Headquarters in Chicago eventually, and ultimately did, rectify that problem as that, had also been noted in other accounts, with the demotion and change of the leadership in 'The Top of the Clock' with that namely being, Jeremiah.

It was a hard and very perplexing war. Again, as I have stated in the beginning, it was a 'fool's war'.

It was a war, that couldn't be won. For that reason, I have stated two things, which I think very important in this portion of this writing. One was, 'minutely agree with'. The other was, 'the genius

Judas that, could have been like, Jesus'. In regard to, 'Minutely agree with', I state that because, although Jeremiah in all probability, was and should be again, minutely, held accountable in many regards as, the one, that many say, was the blame for what had taken place there, during that time. However, on the other side, these were grown men capable of, and with the ability to remember where, they had come from, and granted by right of birth, the ability to as, Nancy Reagan coined the phrase, 'just say no', they of their own volition and free will chose, otherwise.

The other thing was, 'The genius Judas that could have been like Jesus'. The reason that assertion or comparison was made was because, here it was, this man and the gift, blessings and intelligence that he had been bestowed with took an, and that, opportunity to change in a monumental and positive way and have taken seriously, the course of a people that had been long subjugated, shunned and all but excised from, for lack of a better term, the 'normal' society and instead, completely defiled, disgraced and desecrated that gift or opportunity that, was so sorely needed for, and among a people.

The 'Black Mafia'.

I had once overheard a friend from Chicago speaking to another individual in regard to, the gang problem that existed, in the friend's home-town city of, Chicago. I had overheard the friend say to the other individual in regard to an assertion that, "No, that's the Chicago, that the media is telling you about." In regard to Sam Christian and the **'Black Mafia'**, although a vast number of things that the media has told you about, may be true, we will also, go into a number of things that they did not tell you about the **'Black Mafia'** or, it's so called leader or, 'head' of it that, are also true.

From a very close and inside source, I can attest that the formulation of the, **'Black Mafia'** despite what any of the accounts have, can be attributed to one individual by the name of, 'Pork Chop'. Again, as it was relayed to me from a very good and inside source, Richard 'Pork Chop' James was the quintessential portrait in all of its grandiloquence, infamy and demeanor of the picture or, depiction of, a 'gangster'.

"I mean, from the way he dressed, with the big brim cocked to the side. The three-pieced doubled-breasted suits even, to the way he smoked his cigarette or held it in his hands. I mean, when you saw Richard, you immediately had a portrait or vision of say like, an Edward G. Robinson or James Cagney, Humphrey Bogart or somebody, like that. I remember, we were up in this apartment, up in North Philly. It was me, Donny Day, Richard James, Walt, Sam, Ron Harvey, Henry Dabney, Bop Daddy and Nudie. We were counting money, you know. And Sam of course, you know, was in the mirror practicing his quick draw. Everybody else you know, would practice quick draw with one hand. Not Sam though. He had to have two guns. You had to see him. He's like, over in the mirror talking to an imaginary enemy like, 'Yeah, you mother-such and such go ahead, make your move!' That's when Richard said, 'You know what man? We got a strong enough crew right here, to do our own thing. Hell, we ain't really got to be depending on those Guineas. And with all that dope and money that we are getting off of those cats, in the streets and, we already got our own connections. All that we have to do now, is regulate things. Shoot, we can just let them do their thing down there in South Philly and we can do ours up here and, over in West Philly.' And that's how it started." up in, North Philly on that, Sunday. That's about the time when, things began to go quickly to hell in, 'motorized, diamond-studded, tailored-made, money hungry, selfish, greedy, dope filled, hand barrels'.

The brothers had been doing great works at first, on the streets of Philly as well, as in other cities.

Money that had been extracted from the Crap games and the drug dealing at first before, the suggestion of, Richard James in Philly was going to a worthwhile, and very worthy cause, the empowerment of a people. Despite how one may think or feel about it, show me a dollar that's ever been printed, or passed from one hand to another that does not have one's blood sweat or tears on it. Every dollar has blood on it. That fact, unfortunately, but a given, goes all the way back to the thought or idea of, currency as a means, for barter, trade and commerce. That goes from the elected officials voted into office to, the everyday working person. It goes from the currency that we may perchance, give our children for milk money or gifts all the way to, and yes, even the churches.

This, I add for that one person, that was interviewed in that program that made it once again, seem as though, it was the total epitome of blasphemy that one, even a sinner, try to repent for his sins by giving to those in need or places that, those in need, worshipped at.

And they were, getting a lot of money and dope off of the streets too.

At first, everybody was doing the right thing, reporting everything they confiscated, every dollar, every bag of dope. The dope at first, they would destroy. The money of course, was sent to where, it had to go, in Chicago. It was then, soon after Pork Chop's suggestion that it seemed, brothers began feeling the need to, all of a sudden have, the things commensurable with, the position that they had chosen, to take on. That's when, the murders began taking place. Now, all of a sudden, parts or sometimes, all of the dope packages that were confiscated, and ear-marked for prompt and proper destruction so as not to, destroy any more lives, began resurfacing back in the hands of many, of the same people that it was being taken from.

Only difference being now was, it was no longer the product of the people that mayhap originally, put it out there. It was subliminally, in a roundabout, surreptitious, covert way, the property of the newly formed from, the suggestion of Robert 'Pork Chop' James, alleged, *'Black Mafia's'*.

And to make matters worse for the dealers of the product that was formerly, free and clear theirs, if there were any problems like, them being stuck up, robbed or the package was somehow lost, then, that was their problem because they were still indebted to the alleged, *'Black Mafia'* for the cost of that, package.

All of this was done under, and with no doubt to much of the public's eye, as it has been mentioned in the numerous accounts, the watchful and with seemingly, blessings and blind eyes of, Jeremiah. Now, as to whom, and or whether, Sam had actually killed, no matter what is written, the reader is going to leave this read with whatever perception that he, or she decides to believe and leave with in, their minds. But, there is one thing that I want to state in regard to this particular part, that I am writing about now. In regard to the dope that was being re-distributed back onto the streets, I have it, not only a good source, but several very good ones and that is, that Sam never, ever and, to this day, sold drugs.

In fact, in addition to that one, Camel cigarette that he had tried at a very young age and found that smoking was not for him, and the very, very rare few times that he had been known to, have had a drink of anything stronger than water until he, was given cocaine in his later years, after his release from prison and hooked for a very short stint before assistance was given for his recovery by some of the brothers, he had never done or participated in the selling of that dope that is now, or was then, having been, being re-distributed back onto the streets in any shape, form or fashion.

Now once again, as to whether he had actually, taken the life of another, once again, I will leave that to you the reader as, you will of your own volition, surmise or decipher what you will. In that regard, there is one thing that I do know, for certain.

I know that he surely did, kill the hell out of, that pot of pig's feet one day. Going into the kitchen of a party that he had been invited to, and after lifting the lid on a pot that was cooking on the stove there, he turned to Donny at this incident and stated to him, "Look at this! These Lames invited me to a party knowing, I don't eat this crap, and have the nerve to be cooking this stuff on the stove." With that, he then pulled out his 38 revolver from his right side and, 'Blam, blam, blam!'

The party, then seemed more like, a wake as everyone except for those, that had found a very expedient path to the exit way of the front door, then stood around shocked, scared and dumbfounded leaving only, the sound of Smokey Robinson emanating and cajoling throughout as they wondered who, had been the recipient of Sam's wrath in the kitchen.

As the numbers, and scores of deaths and bodies began racking up so too, did the whispers that Sam, and the, alleged, *'Black Mafia'* were, the causes and reasons for them being so. Truth or falsehoods? Again, not doing this to condone or condemn, just telling a story, I'll leave that to you the reader, and your own beliefs and convictions. When things had gotten to the point that they had with drugs, and the profits, from them being introduced into the equation, the hypo-critical insanity caused by it, had gotten to such an extent that, truth, honesty, deception and treachery had become a mottled and muted blur. For the participants involved, it had then, become a hard and oft-times, living and breathing chore to wonder and think that, any day, really, could be one's last amongst, the living.

And like, with the so-called or, alleged, Italian or, other *Mafia*, the real scary and insane factor in that regard was, when summoned, the party summoned had no alternative or choice other than to, an-swer the summons. A great number of people unfortunately, as you already know, had been summoned too.

And the hard, cold truth about that fact too, was that, a lot of those summoned, really never returned or, were seen, or ever heard from again afterwards. Unfortunately again too, and in regard to this fact, as it seemed, it was mostly, mainly and just, outsiders or, 'civilians' that were being summoned and never again heard from again. On the flipside of that and, unfortunately mainly again, a vast number of those doing the summoning were, 'mainly' inclusive of, a number of the brothers that had come from, or had professed to be, members of the Nation of Islam or more to the exact, members of Mosque number 12 or, 'The Top of the Clock'.

With the injection or, 're-injection' of the drugs and the possibility of profit from them, the city that Sam and a number of the brothers from the 'First Resurrection' had brought to together as one, had once again, become fractured and dissected as it once, hell, had always really been, was and was bound to be once again. This is not to take credit from, the admirable effort or illusion of what was, for a brief and short period, achieved.

The 'First Resurrection' is what is commonly known amongst, the general public and those, in The Nation of Islam as, the beginning of, the 'awakening' or, the introduction of, the teachings of The Honorable Elijah to America. They did however as, they had intended to do from the beginning, slow down and in many parts throughout the city, put the brakes on, the youth gang problem in the city. Only problem with that was, that now, many of those former members, desired nothing more than to be, or as near as possible in any shape, form or fashion in emulating or having their names or themselves associated in one regard or the other to, the aura or mystique of the alleged, *'Black Mafia'*. In short, everyone, that used to gang war for nothing and no reasons at all because as lamented in Primacy, (no one, owned the turf that, they had proclaimed to be theirs) wanted to be a gangster, drug dealer or pimp, but very few, wanted to pay the cost to be, the 'Boss'. And, as he went on in 'playing' the part of 'most noble' minister and part time consigliere, this was seemingly, and as it had been perceived and evinced in later years, no doubt fine, with Jeremiah.

For this reason, I have chosen to give the title as such to, this particular chapter about the man who, had helped to assemble a number of mosques and both, a vast amount of older and younger brothers through-out the South and in, the City of Philadelphia. I have also chosen to, title this chapter aptly, and, after a man who once served as spiritual advisor to again also, 'The Greatest of All Time' as, 'The Genius Judas that could have been like, Jesus.' In regard to Sam himself, it was also around this time that he, had been elevated to the point in the eyes and minds of both, law-enforcement and the general public to that of, some sort of, malevolent golem or apparition that you did not want to, or dare see lest, risk the possibility of, not being able to see or, breathe again.

Looking back now, I guess that he had in fact, in a number of ways or respect become, to a number of people, those two delineations that, I had just previously described, in some certain aspects or ways. On that note, to evince that point, two incidents in particular come to mind.

There was this one incident, when I say again, looking back now, I guess, that he was supposedly, or was supposed to had been, 'on the run' and was walking out of a house in North Philly with Donny. In regard to those last statements, I am pretty certain that you will see why I had previously stated, 'supposedly' and 'I guess' after I relay this next part. He and Donny had just walked out of this house in North Philly and had encountered outside of the house, two Philadelphia detectives that were on the corner up the street from, there.

Sam had not seen the two detectives at first as he, and unknowingly to Donny also, had been walking directly, in the direction that the detectives were located at on, this particular corner. As they had approached the detectives, Donny being the first to notice them, whispered surreptitiously out of the side of his mouth to Sam, "Yo man, you see 'em right there?" Sam, unable to afford, and not even a millisecond off of, the observation then, without looking at Donny and, with his own voice, just a pitch above a whispering responds, to Donny while, with his eyes dead on directly, at the detectives, "Yeah, I see 'em." "What, you gonna do? I mean, you already know my feelings, we gonna have it out right here, or what? Let me know because, I'm gonna start reaching right now." "Nah, hold up. Let's just keep walking and see how they feel. Let's see what, they wanna do first." With that, as they then came up upon the two detectives who, it seemed had decided that, it wasn't in their best interest to challenge he and Donny, one of them, with a shy half step, leans in Sam 's and Donny's direction. With that, and there, far enough only, and alone, he then, states to them, "Hold up, wait, we're not here to arrest you. Sam, we just wanted you to know that, you must have a lot of people in this city that really, like you. We knew where, you were, but we couldn't get anyone in the city to tell us that or, anything else. That's all we wanted to, say to you. You gentleman have a nice day." With that, the two detectives then, let Donny and Sam proceed on their way in the direction that they were going which, happened to have entailed, right past the detectives as they, did likewise, on their way back to their precinct, I presume.

On that note, I am reminded of an incident that Donny, had re-layed to me about when Sam once, chased an adversary into a police precinct and first, after continuing on, then finished, firing on him, right there.

Of course, and once again, all this was a time before, they would send, a whole police force to converge and descend upon one indi-vidual for say, selling, 'Loosy's' or, loose cigarettes. And too, I guess those two detectives knew that, in all probability that, the chances they, would have fared very well up against he and Donny were at best, slim to none, had they tried to engage the two of them in gun play before, their back-up would have arrived.

Then, there was the other time in the city when there was a meet-ing that took place of among all of the major 'gangster' players or again, the alleged members of the so called again, alleged, *'Black Mafia'*.

As stated earlier, a vast number of murders had been taking place in, and throughout the city after many of the brothers both, from within, and outside of 'The Top of the Clock' found more enchanting, enamoring and profitable, the lucrativeness of the drug game. In fact, the streets and the game had become so vicious then, that even, Richard 'Pork Chop' James, the one who had, come up with the idea, invent and title for, the alleged, *'**Black Mafia**'* had become one, of its victims.

During this particular meeting, three individuals that were unknown to anybody from within the meeting or city, had entered the meeting, as well. Being 'strapped to the teeth', after entering the meeting, one of the three simply asked one question. "Is anybody here named, Donny Day?" Answering up, Donny then says, "Yeah, that's me." The individual that made the inquiry then says to Donny, "You can leave." Of course, at this, you can imagine the reaction of many of those, in attendance at this particular meeting. This was so because, Donny was specifically and particularly 'summoned' or, had been requested, to be in attendance at this particular meeting.

Yes, the one and the same, Donny Day. Donny Day, Sam's 'main, main man!', Brother Hamid. His man, whose mother, had verbally reflected privately to him that, "You even seem to, walk better when you're with Sam." Donny Day, by most accounts of street lore and legend by those whom, had never met him stood, just shy of say about, 6' feet and 5" inches. The actual truth was however, in actuality, Donny Day stood a hair, just above, 5' feet and 7" inches if, that. Also again, by some certain accounts of that same lure and legend, when you saw him, on one side of him at a certain time of day, it seemed almost like, the certain hue of, a certain time of day when, the day was bending towards, an indigo blue shade. On the other side there it seemed, was a light likened to that of, the hue, of the morning sunshine and its rays. I guess, what could be taken into consideration or construed was, the fact that being, a former welter-weight champ in the Pennsylvania

Penal System, it could also be considered prudent to think that, he had in effect in deed and, in fact, or in some sort of a way, the benefit of being able to have had, in his possession, the power, authority or ability of actually, granting the light of day, or darkness of the night over some individuals.

And even though I had those, few cross words with Donny, it was not as if I first, didn't know about or had forgotten that fact, and also or, as if, I would have had, in any sort of way, any sort in the sense of a win if things, would have escalated further than those, words. That was in regard to Donny himself irrespective, of any other thing that, he could have done or, had done to, me.

Then again, even if I had developed that inclination to, seep or ease into in my mind, after coming to have known Donny as I had, the hardest fight, that I would have had with Donny would have been to, not have been broken up or, dying from the laughter at his glib, and realistic view of, to me, damn near any, and everything.

That feeling had been wrought in upon our, his and mine's first meeting of his ability in laughter, or jocularity, to make one find, the same and clarity of perception in any, or everything that he had, and or would, speak about.

Now, as a testament to the relationship between him and Sam and the reciprocation of his love, admiration, brotherhood and respect in turn. I recall once again, that conversation which, had taken place when Donny's character and his proclivities and what they had meant to Sam, had been called into question. That was when Sam had stated to the other party and had also, in advance, before that other party could even think about formulating any responses, straightened out any questions in possible retort that, "Don't ever worry about this brother! When it's time to do what has to be done, I know he's on point!" This was Sam's man whose name, had become synonymous with his own. Yes, this was the same guy who, upon our first meeting, had struck me with upon many other things, his articulateness.

Not only Sam's man, but his, main man! A great number of things, had started happening.

They had started happening as, I had stated earlier, quickly too, and they were not happening for the good, or, in a good way either. Sam, had noticed these happenings as, well.

Unknown to the cast that were in attendance at this particular meeting though was, that he, had known about this meeting too, as well. He had also, noticed, and taken note of the very fast and even more, vast decline of 'loyalty' that had been as of late, coming out.

Although again, as he had professed to wanting to be nothing more than, a soldier, he had before the 'First Resurrection' understood, the rules to, the 'game'.

'You don't kill off your assets'. That was a luxury that, was reserved for, your enemies. You negotiate, you bargain, you deal with and, you utilize with, or, them.

The Jolly Green Giant, 'Hershel Williams' who had been eliminated during the month of, November in, 1975 was not an enemy. He was not of the Brotherhood inside of the Brotherhood of the organization, but he was an earner, and he was considered to be, loyal to his charge, with his associates. He was still however, one of the brothers, and he could have been made to, or reasoned with, in lieu of what, was eventually his, or, that final outcome, which was his demise.

Maybe their reasons and thoughts might have been along the lines of thinking as that of, many of the others of Sam's associates or, 'Brothers' around that time. They were the many whom, had figured or assumed that, since he, Sam was and would be, off of the 'radar' or, 'on the bench' that he mayhap or, might eventually, come around to a point of acceptance in regard to those, that were now becoming, rash, brash and careless actions of others by the time, that he, would be back into a position that in reality, he had never really, left.

When Hershel's demise came, and in the way that it was done (in the presence of his children whom had seen it happen and after, coming out of church), Sam knew that, loyalty to, and of the thing that was put together if ever, there was truly a thing called, The **Black Mafia** was lost.

From where he was, Sam even knew, of the underlying reason, for the meeting that was taking place.

There were a sparse few conviction-filled, but not too loud, or austere and staunch verbal ramblings of retort to the request or 'permission', of the three's spokesperson. Hell, even Donny at first, was a little bit confounded so, despite the request or, granting of 'leave', he stayed or, stuck around as even, the spokesperson of the three knew, he would.

To the subtle ramblings, the spokesperson then, with a great mixture of cordiality and command stated politely, "Hold up! Hold up brothers! We didn't come here to cause any conflict or confusion. We only came here at the behest, and request as a favor, for a brother. You have a phone in here with an intercom and conference system right?" The room then stirred with a mild, but not so much like, a rush, but whisk or breeze of mild astonishment and non-verbal inquisitiveness at the spokesperson's knowledge of the intercom phone system.

One of the brothers present in the meeting then, went and retrieved the phone for the stranger.

Now the odd or strange part that took place happened after, the brother had brought the intercom system for the phone back into the room.

This was so because, after the phone was brought back into the room, the spokesperson of the three, did not reach or touch it to, dial a number. Instead, he, and the other two that were with him, after relaying to everyone in the meeting that, everything was alright and that everyone in the room should calm down as all things would surely, be explained, he sat down right before the phone. With-in five minutes after the stranger had done that, the phone rang.

Normally, the sound of a phone ringing would, garner no more than, a cursory glance or, a request for someone to answer it. However, given the unusual intrusion and request of the strangers on this particular day, the otherwise, disruptive ring may have just as well, had been ringing from the confines of City Hall resounding, all the way up Broad Street to this, their one, of many particular meeting spots. To boot, it may have as well, come at three a.m. in the morning with everyone including, those in attendance at the meeting asleep. This was mainly so because, of the way that all who, were in attendance at the meeting, and in serious anticipation of the call, that would explain everything were seemingly, startled or jolted at, the ringing of it.

On the second ring, the spokesperson of the three strangers picked up the receiver and answered.

"Yes. Yes sir, my brother. He's still here. Yes, we did tell him." The spokesperson for the three then pressed the button that read, 'conference'. With the now lighted button on the phone system showing a luminescence and hue equaled to that of, a sixty watt light bulb, the meeting then, had really, outside of and having overshadowed the one that, certain parties, may have had in mind, commenced.

Although someone else, and possibly, no, for sure, for nefarious reasons called the meeting, the un-expected and un-invited voice on the other end of the receiver was the one, as it now came to light, that had taken charge of it.

"I'm fully aware of what's been going on. And, I'm also aware of why, this meeting was called." It was up until this point before, the voice on the other end of the receiver had spoken that Donny, like the others, had been pretty much, clueless as to, the reason for the interruption by the three strangers.

After making a few cordial greetings to a number of brothers that were in the room, and returning a few icy and standoff-ish greetings towards some of the others, he then, got into the matter at hand, which had precipitated him making this particular call, in the first place.

As, he was winding down with his input and instructions on just, 'what was what' he concluded his call with a serious word of advice to all who were present, that was most important for them all to, really listen to, and consider.

"I just want to make it clear to everyone here that, Donny is my brother. I'm fully aware of the thoughts, that some of you, may have had in mind. And I just want it also, to be known that, if anything happens to Donny and I mean, anything. If he trips on the sidewalk. If he slips in the shower or, if he cuts himself shaving. I mean, anything, your best hope is that he himself, tells me that, that is what happened. Because, if he doesn't, I'm going to take it as a personal attack against me. So, now, that we have that part of your meeting out of the way, you can continue on, with it. But, before you do, I want you all to keep this one thing, in mind. ***Remember, we have had this meeting so that, your family does not have to dress up for the next one."*** To this, he added, "I'm talking especially, to you, Lonny and Ronny!" With that, he was speaking of, and both to, Ronald (Harvey) and Lonnie (Dawson). With the inclusion of those two names towards the end of his call, he was letting all in the room know, exactly who it was, that had caused him to show that irrespective of his present where-about, and or predicament that as shown, and evinced, in the muscle that had been sent to the meeting that, any and everybody in that room, were not out of the reach of his grasp should he, had decided that, he had wanted to reach out and touch them. ***"Are we understood?"***

To that, he knew, he did not need, and nor, was he really expecting a response because everyone present that day knew, without a minis-cule of doubt, understood fully, and would comply. As I have touched upon earlier in a roundabout way in writing this part, this meeting had taken place in or about, around, 1975. Sam had been away, and had just begun, in the confines of the penal system of New York State, his time on a sentence of, 15 years to life. The three men or 'shooters' that he had summoned to the meeting, were out of Detroit where, he had also, by that time, blazed a path, or his name, had been well circulated around, and in certain, incendiary and serious circles.

"What we're gonna do now," as promised earlier, *"is, go back".*

'Samuel Richard Carter & the Greatest 'Magic' trick that, the world has ever 'Not', 'witnessed'. '

On, April 1st, 1972, the weather vane at the closest, Philadelphia weather station, which was, the Philadelphia International Airport listed conditions as a high, in the temperature of 59 degrees. The low for that day, was listed to be at a cool, 39 degrees. In Atlantic City, from the nearest weather vane, conditions there, were logged in as a mildly, and fickle breeze in the high of a temperature of just at, 51 degrees. Being close to the water, the temperature that evening came in at just under a tenth of, a foolishly and a fickle, 29 degrees. It was that season of the year in and around that geographical location where it was allowed, and even sometimes expected, for the season to have that fancifully fickle and foolish feel and or, effect of both, over the inhabitants and location of that particular geographical area of the environ or map of the seasons dissected over the globe.

Growing up in one area, and having spent, dreamed, and reflected on the time again, spent in the other, one could even also, go so far as to, the extent of feeling emboldened or even deservedly, and rightfully earned, of the fanciful fleeting giddy, and foolish feeling that, was especially caused, and felt, in that particular geographical area of the environ during, that particular time of the season. That was so because, in that particular area, and during that particular time of the season, as many of the true inhabitants of that particular environ, have at one time or another, had that feeling or, do experience that feeling, or sensation. It was the one that provided, or gave off the real assistance or resonance to that giddily fleeting and foolish feeling or sensation conjured or brought up, for one, in that particular geographical locale of, and in the entire of the whole geographical spin of the seasonal and its changes as well as, things and thoughts caused or conjured up by the, or those, changes.

In that particular area, or environ, it was one where, it gave one, the giddy and fleeting sensation of a feather, being caught between the soft winds and currents of daylight as likened to that, in the prospective perspective with the promise of warmth, a light exemplary breeze or taste of the blissfulness of the coming summer winds, or months and, the harshly cold, and numbing reality of that, which still, had to be weathered as, the almost insanely soothing day-light longing and the almost, woeful, morose and mournful reminder of, the reverberating uncertain feeling brought on with the night, of the cool and almost, cold darkness of the uncertainty, and unknowing of, what possibly, may, might or will happen in that again, on-coming and cold night as payment or recompense for, future or past deeds done selfishly on behalf, or in regard to one's self.

A befittingly titled, or so named day, on this particular date in, April and on, the 1st of, 1972 for certain participants and the great number of others, was it aptly called. In many of the other geographical locations without regard to, the season or seasonal changes of definitive or defining emotions or attributes of the individuals or inhabitants of those particular environs or locales again aptly, the day was called, 'All Fools Day' or, 'April Fool's Day'. Once again, coming from that particular geographical area or environ between, Philadelphia and the Jersey shore such days like that, which that region was experiencing then, and without regard to, that particular connotation or jocularly named title, that the day was called, many could still, be expected to have had or, experience a certain quirky or foolish type, in a good way, dysphoria or sensation caused as the result of such days as that, which the region was on, or around that date, experiencing. It was the one where, in the day-light hours one could sometimes, become wrapped up and enraptured again, by the prospect or promise of the positive and fanciful almost child-like, wishing or, whimsical foretelling of a prosperous future or season to come, in the ensuing months. Then once again also, on the evening side, there was that portentously foreboding cold and dark awakening or reminding to one, of that, which still, had to be endured.

However, if one had access to enough monetary and liquid assets, he or she, for a time, and sometimes fallaciously could either, enhance or prolong for a period, that confidently bright and oft-times, childishly and foolish sunny and promising outlook or dispositions experienced in those daylight hours. That was especially true, in and around that particular geography or locales between Philadelphia and Atlantic City and other northeastern regions also around, that time.

Like both, the Schuylkill River and the Atlantic Ocean in between the areas of Philadelphia, the Jersey Shores and Atlantic City around that time, a lot of money was starting once again, to flow.

This in turn fooled, and lulled, an even greater number of people in those particular areas into, that false sense of, assuredness topped with that promise of, positivity and or, prosperity.

The next day of course was, April the 2nd. On this date, in 1972, the closest available weather station capable of recording the temperature in and around the City of Brotherly Love, came from the Willow Grove Naval Air Station up and around, the top end of Route 611 just after the tip of Broad Street. The temperature or high there, for that day was, and at that particular weather station, recorded temperatures in the region at a calm, 50 degrees. It was a cool nine degrees shy than it was, the previous day. The low recorded for the evening there, was at, 37.9 degrees. That shied at just, a scant 1.1 degree than, the previous evening, there. In Atlantic City, as now evinced, the weather station there, was located at or, recorded from, The Atlantic City International Airport, there. The daylight temperature there, in Atlantic City that day, was recorded at, a breezy 48.9 degrees down

there by, the ocean. That was a light 2.1 degrees just shy of the temperature that was recorded there, the previous day. The low for the
evening there, was listed or recorded at just, a short 5 degrees above,
the freezing point.

Contrasting and incongruent to the previous evening there when,
the record was listed as being, a couple of degrees lower by a cooler,
8.1 degrees. That next day in itself and, as being what it was, no matter what the exact date, that it may have particularly fell on, had in its
own a sort of, 'All Fool's Day' feel to it although, that too, was in a
different sort of feel or way. On that particular date in 1972, the next
day was, Easter Sunday.

If you were born in an urban or city environ, then you can especially relate to, the almost foolishly, and childish-like fanciful magical
feelings or sensations that, were wrought up on, and about with, the
festivities and rituals on that particular date, and day as, well.

'Omega by the Sea'

For the young and young at heart, which on this particular day
seemed, to be inclusive of practically, everyone as they would all, be
outfitted, and bedecked about, in their newly for-this-particular-day
purchased spring ensembles and suits.

It magically and seemingly, provided that just and right needed
spark. That one again, which foolishly and childishly excited or, was
the cause or precipitant of one to, whether, erroneously or not, be
filled with that promise of either coming fortunes or continual pros-
perities. This phenomenal, was not just one that was, or only, felt by
either, the young or the old either. Rather again, it was one that, was
inclusive of all, both, the young and old. Again, being from the urban confines from such a city as Philly, as many may know, after first
tending, and then attending to the ritualistic portions and autonomies
of this particular holiday, what many folks liked, to do.

Those things on that day, that first needed tending to were, the adherence to what as many, of the brothers would believe, that which, was taught by the virtues and propaganda of the slave masters and most mothers. That was first, one's attendance in church for the so-called, celebration of the 'rising', of Jesus Christ from the dead after being 'crucified', on a cross.

Then after that, there was the tending to, the festive side or portion of the day, which entailed, not just one's own (if one had them), but a more than a moderate amount or slew of other neighborhood children or 'passer-byers'. Finally, after tending to all that, what many again from such urban environs liked to do was, hop in their freshly cleaned 'rides' or cars, and 'get out of town' if not, for an all-night sabbatical then, for a good couple of hours, at least.

For many, and for many years, Atlantic City had provided for just this type, or sort of fast relief in getting away or, 'one-night' sabbatical.

For Tyrone, 'Mr. Millionaire' Palmer, it was no different. He was, as evinced from his association with Frank Matthews, one of those, 'Money Makers'. Then, places like, the Latin Casino or Club Harlem were famous in helping to provide, that much needed relief, or help in reducing, the stresses from the everyday ubiquity of the city.

Also back then, one other venue where, a great number of people liked to flock to down there was a place called, 'Omega by the Sea'. If one may recall, that was the precursor to a venue that briefly, used to take place in Philly called, 'The Greek Festival', which was held for a very brief period at a place called, the Belmont Plateau in Fairmount Park, there. Many may also recall, the story of how, that venue was terminated or brought to an end too.

Billy Paul who, used to when, back in his home-town of Philly, frequent Adele's Restaurant on, 15th & South right along with, and like, Sam and a large host of others from Stars to, gangsters and regular everyday people was, the performing head-lining act, as it had been told, a million times over and in just as an, equal amount of different ways at Club Harlem there, on this particular, Easter Sunday.

Also, as it had been told a million times over, he had just begun with his opening song. Had he, finished the first verse of the number, given all the things that had transpired from that point, it would have seemed, an almost magical, prophetic, poetical and capable of being terminal, verse.

As he began, "I like to dream yes, right between my sound machine." it was then, that something took place seemingly worthy of the admiration of either, Blaine or Copperfield as shots began to, ring out, just off the stage where, Billy would have finished, 'On a cloud of sound, I drift into the night. Any place it goes, is right. Goes far, flies near to the stars, away from here.' There has been a great number of things written and said in regard to this incident, and the events surrounding it. Yes, and as promised if only, for the desire of satisfying my own need to know, I then asked the questions that many have long, been desiring to know, in regard to exactly what, had transpired and the reasons behind it, on that day.

In the interim since we had begun writing, also we, he and I had grown to, a far and more profound brotherly state beyond that of, a great many of those who would, or could consider themselves as being, a part of, or having knowledge of, or had heard rumors or, have had some interactions with the likes of, Sam Christian. With that bestowal, never lost or negated too, was the knowledge or astuteness in knowing not only the importance of these, his spoken words, but also too, the thirst or anxiousness of a public, to finally, hear them.

"Was it about the drugs or, the Frank Matthews thing or, the money involved with it, that the media talks about?"

His openness and candor as he responded despite, our own solidly forged bond, was almost chilling in a surreal sort of way. I know, a great deal of this feeling that, I was feeling at this, was due in part, because I was not only actually sitting here, with this man that, I and you, the reader had been wondering, and wanting to inquire either of, or about, for years. But also too, I was sitting there inquiring about, despite whatever other delineations that one may perchance, put on it, such a monumental portion or clip in time and the history of, 'The City of Brotherly Love'.

"No, it wasn't about any of those things. It was personal."

Upon hearing that, did I convict him as, others had? In the interest of integrity and truth while, out of respect for the bond or feelings of adoration that, had grown between us, I feel it best served now that, if my own objective or deducible mind remain, or be deferred from, opinionating or making that judgment now, or ever to you, the reader. That aside, I still like others, given the information and rumors or, versions of the situation had along with them, that deep penetrating interest and desire to know that one very important thing, that they had also, longed and wanted to know.

Unlike them though, yet as well, and for them, along with, in the interest of truth and integrity, I had the opportunity and ability to 'ask'. So, I eagerly, took full advantage of the opportunity for them, as well as myself, when I asked that which myself, and both those many others, longed for so long, to finally, be able to ask of him and know the answer to when I inquired, "Brother Beyah, I have to ask." **"Ask away, ain't that, what you're here for?"**

"They say, it was almost eight-hundred people there that night and yet, you were found not guilty. I mean, I understand the things that people say in regard to, the power of power and, the capabilities of some people. I've even, also heard it mentioned about, or have been made aware of, a great many of the people that were alleged to have been, or that were actually associated with you. But, there's something that's been eating at my brain."

At this point, to coin a statement made later by the judge in one, of the most major and important cases in Sam's life, Justice Burton Roberts, I did, "not see any militants or monsters breaking down the doors or scaling down from the ceiling" coming to kill me or to, whisk him away.

"In regard to Atlantic City, I know for a certainty even, as I could imagine at that time, and my young age at that time, that people, from as far away as, Baltimore or even, New York would, and often did, travel there, to Club Harlem just, on a whim. And for such a top notch and head-lining act as Billy Paul was at that time, I'm almost certain too, or would have been inclined to believe that, for that particular, or such a show that, there may have been or actually were, some people that did, travel from that far away as those places just mentioned to, want to have seen him, performing. I mean, not even Hitler, Genghis Khan or, Kim Il Sung had that much power that stretched so far as to, given the gravity of just such a situation, not have one individual to, stand up in defiance or objection of the things or atrocities that were said to have, or actually had, happened."

Looking back now, and with more than, twenty-twenty hindsight bias, and given, the plethora of details and information that I had been granted and given privy to along with, the details of that yet to be expounded upon, I am forced and compelled now, to see the naivety or obtuseness of that un-intelligent, or haste to prejudge, observation.

For as you, the astute reader may have already surmised, or will soon also surmise, that yes, there was an aura or, that strong 'state of being' within and around Sam and those, that were associated with him that had extended, just that far.

"So, you mean to tell me that, the alleged, **Black Mafia** had that much power, which extended all the way to that point where, not one witness came forth to say that it was you?"

Never acknowledging, accepting or conceding to, the existence of the alleged, **Black Mafia** and without missing a beat, and also, without a hint or trace of any of the ethos or things said about, or that would be thought to, have been associated with such an individual, he then responded to me in a manner likened to that, of someone, having just had survived a harrowing experience or, of one, having just come into a sudden windfall of good fortune when he responded to that query with, *"All I can say to that is, Al-Hum-du-Allah for both my lawyer, Albert Fillipone and my judge, Adrian Bernelli who was, a devout catholic, and one of the most humane people, that God, had ever made!"*

Then there, as Tyrone, 'Mr. Millionaire' Palmer had, 'faded into the night and far away from here.' and as promised to you, the reader and for the sake of integrity, I then, and finally, asked the question of Sam that again, many people (including, myself) have been, and pardon the pun, 'dying' to hear the answer to.

"Did you do it?"

Without answering, but with a look on his face, that left no room for any more questions as I had pondered on my next question it read to me that, *'Some things truly are, between a man and his creator despite, others desires, thirsts and dire needs just for the sake of self-appeasement to, know.'*

Although, I may sound, or seem glib and insensitive in my writing and this point, I want to make or, re-iterate a very important thing that must again, be noted. But before that, I want to expound on the 'why' or 'personal' reasons as to why, as I had found out both, through Sam, and those several other reliable sources on what had transpired in Atlantic City did as, it most definitely, and unequivocally did, transpire .

Although a great number of the other law-enforcement and news or expose' sources and stories had it and mainly true that eventually, it had become all about the money and the drugs, in this particular incident, it was in fact, as Sam had stated, a good deal more personal.

One of Sam's close and personal friends by the name of, James 'P.I.' Smith had been murdered for whatever the reason shortly before, the incident or event in Atlantic City took place. When the incident took place, whomever was sent or had went to Atlantic City, had gone there to speak with 'Mr. Millionaire' in regard to, P.I.'s murder.

Now, what many had failed, or had been forced by the volley of gunshots in the main hall to take into consideration was that while, or during the attempt to speak with, 'Mr. Millionaire' had been taking place, in one of the bathrooms off of the main hall, an argument or heated exchange of words had ensued. *It was in there first where, there were shots that, were exchanged.*

Again, not to seem glib or insensitively insolent, but after that took place, I guess that any attempts at discussion had then, at that particular point, become a moot point or, to use a commonly used term in such places as that of, Atlantic City or Las Vegas, *'All bets were off'.*

It was then that, everything then became, a mystery or magic trick deserving of either, the likes of the song that, Billy Paul had begun into, the first verse of singing or, of the two, David's. Those being, David Blaine or David Copperfield.

Again, it is not that I do not have any compassion or that, I don't feel or see as, what took place in Atlantic City that night as, a tragedy. Nor, is it that I don't feel as though, the loss of life including that of, Tyrone Palmer had not, has not, or did not hold any value, as also, I think that, every life is important. It is only that, I think it fair, to keep things in their proper context. To do that, one has to consider that, given the things or 'game' that, they (that being inclusive of each, and every one of them and those today, that decide to, make that decision) were involved in, every one of them knew, or should know or have known, been and or, be made aware of that which, they were, and or, are choosing, to become involved in.

And as my condolences and heart sincerely, goes out to the families and loved ones of the victims, unfortunately, that is a sad fact, that I am certain was, or should not have been, lost on them.

The point that I am strongly endeavoring to make here is that, in that 'game', which was, and continues to be played and the things that were and are done in conjunction with the choices that were, and are made, each and every one them, those women included in Atlantic City were, and are involved in a game that was and is still, so nefarious and evil that, it was then, and is again still, a game where, there were, and could again, never, be any 'real' winners.

It was, and is a game that, as time has taught, and does teaches, that for the players involved, there can only quickly be two outcomes despite the very rare few that last, or exist for a minute period longer than most of the others that may choose to be, or may become involved in it, no matter in, what the capacity that being, the supplier or demander of, it.

I am guessing now, that, this is why, and as it has been again relayed to me by, a good deal of those reliable sources close to him, that Sam, placed very little if any value at all, on a thing that as explained earlier, existed long before, and that he knew, would continue and exist long after him other than for, the 'help' and to further, the cause that he, and the Nation of Islam had first, set out to do.

As he, and I have discussed and agreed upon, this was despite, or in spite of the fact that, in this, there was the dichotomy or paradox that he, and the many others before and since, were certain although, as history has, and still continually evinces otherwise, that they were doing so futilely, that he, and those before him, thought that he, or that they, could succeed in overcoming.

'No baby is born a devil, it's a learned behavior.'

In a vast number of the things that we had discussed, Sam would oft-times, inject this statement. Whether, it was in the cause of either doing something on the side of good or, for one's own selfish or nefarious needs or deeds, if that party's convictions were that strong or, set upon doing whatever it was that they mayhap, been desiring to achieve, it is my belief that, it required one of either three types of individuals.

That individual had to either, had the heart of a true soldier or, had been one with, no heart at all. Then there was, the last or, lastly, one besieged with the mind of a true, 'mad man'. In regard to the latter, this meant, that such an individual in this regard, was one that in all actuality, and honesty, was one that, had to have been bordering on the side of being certifiably, in need of some serious medication as well as, a commitment to a psychiatric facility-sick-in-the-head insane.

On January 18th, 1973, seven men from Philadelphia as it had been written and spoken about, all had gotten into two vehicles and headed south on I-95 with, destination of, Washington D.C. in mind.

I don't think that I have to re-hash or re-tell the whole tragic story as, I'm quite certain that, in one form, fashion or other, that many of you, have heard most, of the sordid details involving the incident of which, I am now going to add an observation or opinion on. And in particular of, one certain individual there, in particular in regard to, the events that took place on, that fateful and sad day. Upon reaching their destination in D.C., the seven individuals then, got out of the two vehicles that they had driven there in, and embarked upon a house there, that was said to have been purchased and owned by, basketball great, Kareem Abdul Jabbar formerly known as, Lew Alcindor

After the seven individuals then, made their entrance into the home there, the exact same number of occupants that were inside of the home, consisting of, five children and two adults were then brutally, murdered.

I inquired of Sam on, just as you too, wanted to know, his thoughts or feelings on what had transpired there upon, that fateful event, and day.

If it is now, one's desire or still, the seeking of the melodramatic that is being sought after, or yearned to be fulfilled, then now, be it not, my responsibility or blame for the disappointment in that seeking or desire. And now, if wonderment or the thoughts, in one's mind of whether, his thoughts and feelings would be of like-mindedness paralleling or, along the path of thinking with one's own thus leading to, that revelation becoming one of shock to said individual, then once again, I hope that this revelation does not become one, of earth-shattering proportions in one's thoughts or feelings either.

For, I found it not only refreshing, but rather more of, a relief to have found that, they were right along the same lines of thinking again, along with both, 'yours, as well as mine's.'

"Brother Beyah, in regard to that situation that took place in D.C., you know, the Hanafi killings, what are your feelings and take on it?" It was then, that first time when, I could truly recall really although he had said it a number of times, hearing it as when, and with the **inflection** and **adamancy** in his voice and tone, as he responded, *"No baby is born a devil, it's a learned behavior!"* Comfortable and feeling that, sense of satisfaction and ease ebbing up and upon me, I pressed further, *"I mean what do you think in regard to the,"* not knowing how, or which way to term them I finished, *"guys who committed those acts?"*

Using the term, 'committed' was in an effort or, a thinly veiled attempt to disguise, or hide my perplexity or ardent inability of being able to understand or find a way of formulating in my mind as to how, that I could grasp or truly, in my own heart to call, the perpetrators of this or, these acts, *'brothers'* and not wanting to offend him should, he had found, felt or, commiserated them as, 'right' in their actions or cause'. At the same time, the thing that I dreaded the most, was in my own heart and mind.

I was fearful or, dreaded of being unable to go on with him, inside of my own heart and mind let alone, for as, far as to, and for the sake of this story had those, or that last thought been his actual feelings as well, of them still being, worthy or able, of being called, *'brothers'*.

Because then to me, inside of my mind, and all that I hold or held sacred as knowledge, wisdom, peace and contentment along with, understanding in regard to him, and other things in life as well, as all of the things that I have heard associated with regard to him, and the other things in this world, would have been to me, of monumental proportions, an earth-shattering lie.

That again, was because to me, that thought was in all of the things that I had thought, or thought that I had been through, the one constant that kept me precariously bound to in my mind, the precarious precipice of sanity.

And then, there was, that other thing that had become of such monumental importance to me. In fact, it had become of pinnacle importance to me. Despite, all that I had promised myself and you, as the reader in my obligation as a writer that, I have been and am determined to fulfill, I had come to, in the most ardent brotherly and family sense of the term, love Sam. That was especially so for me because mainly, I had gotten to see parts of the man that not even this story, could discern. And also, I had gotten to see them without any fears, suspicions or trepidations from the man.

We were not, and are not necessarily defined, but rather, we are shaped and molded by our circumstances and experiences. It was true that, *'no child was born a devil, it was a learned behavior.'*

"To me, that was the act of a scared man or crazy man! No baby is born a devil! It's a learned behavior!" was, and again, I was glad for it, his thoughts and response to my query on this part of his story. Later, although he would apply this sentiment in explaining many, of the other transitions, plateaus and destinations that he would eventually reach in this world and life, then, and at this particular time and juncture, he expressed it, and meant it in, it's most literal sense, of the terms.

I can't help but to think that, there was a certain air or physiognomic desire to stress a point sort of feeling, or sense swirling about him later, when he elaborated a little more in regard to his feelings on that incident, which had transpired there, in Washington D.C. . I guess, the closest thing that I could relate or, equate it to, was one sort of like, a sense of 'Prophecy or, 'cies' being or, finally, having been fulfilled.

If that description seems a bit broad for some, then I think a better one, that many can best relate to is, one sort of more like, 'See, I told you so!'. That was the first, only and closest time that, I would say in regard to the term, 'arrogance' in, and with regard to, Sam. This time, that seeming sense was marked also, on his face with a hint of a smirk or smile of gloating satisfaction of being happy to have as opportunity, something so profound to show as proof or, example. However, it did not, even then, seem, in a self-serving or self-aggrandizing type, or sort of way, arrogance.

This observation was noted during, his lamenting or gloating on, when he, had first gotten word about, and was discussing with one of the other very important brothers that, as I had promised, I would also speak about, and of his monumental importance in Sam's life, were talking about how, and the circumstances of when, one of the main perpetrators of those murders died while, in prison, of a massive heart attack.

To the outside observer, as it would have seemed, a conversation so casual, as two individuals discussing something as ephemerally unimportant as either, a sporting event or, a game of pool. But, between the two of them, as I had learned, was it of monumental and eternal importance, and worth the attention paid to it!

"They say, old boy don't look too good, up there!" It was then, as he looked over his shoulder and I saw as, he was relaying that portion of the conversation that took place with the other brother, the reason for this aura, air or, sensing in his actions of his, physiognomic desire to express 'arrogantly', something profound. It was then again, as he had in the past, and would continually do, when desiring, or stressing something valuable to be taken from what he was saying as he looked me directly, in the eyes and stated, ***"Then, he died of a massive heart attack the very next day after me, and the brother were just, talking about it!"*** that, I understood better, this suddenly expressed display of, or what I had thought to be, arrogance. It was because, as and in the way that, he looked back at me while elaborating on this fact and point, he looked and seemed almost, relieved, happy or even, excited or, 'arrogant' to have as example or proof, to a might, or power other than, or outside of that which many, had attributed or, had come to equate, to himself or, the 'aura' of, Sam Christian.

In it, that look, he looked, and seemed, almost vindicated. He looked almost vindicated to be able to have or, to show that example to, someone. He looked all at once both, vindicated and relieved to have and show as example, a true, cut directly from the story of his, Sam Christian's larger than life it self's life, to show, and share a story of how, an insanely sick-in-the-head and misguided individual with seemingly again, no heart or, scared man ***had found*** meaning, in all three, in the end.

He had found his sanity, through his guilt and conscience. Then too, and two, he had then found, his heart although in that, he had found it both, the physically literal and metaphorically sense. In that again, he had found it from, the guilt and conscience as they both failed, and gave out on him, his physical heart and his physical mind that would never, ever again be, with any thoughts that would again, ever concern any others with that, the expiration of his last breath.

It was then again, at that point in his relaying this particular portion of the story to me that, he had again, reiterated, and re-affirmed his understanding of karma, prophecy or, of a, no, that power higher than he or, what others had tried or again, had attributed to him, as he once again, exclaimed upon his initial exclamation or heralding of that statement, *"No baby is born a devil! It's a learned behavior!"* Be it suffice to say that, this is, and was Samuel 'Beyah' Christian's take on what had transpired in Washington D. C. on that fateful and tragic day of, January, 18th 1973.

When a baby does something incongruent to societal standards or norms we sometimes correct with, mild physical chastisement you know, like the bible says, *'Spare the rod and spoil the child', 'Proverbs: 13;24'.*

Then, when the baby becomes of the age or, the time of cognizance we, correct with advice just as in, you know like, the Quran says.

After that then, well, it's just that, *"No, baby is born a devil, it's a learned behavior!"* That sentiment or feeling holds especially true, in regard to the ones, not even given the benefit of cognizant thought process.

Once again, choices. Although, as horrendous in and of itself which, that crime was, it pales in comparison to, this next and most important thought on that incident.

The fact that, there were *babies* involved, and those *babies* were never even given, that choice or, chance at, cognitive thinking. Ultimately, and, as it mayhap have been or be, for you, as it has, was and is for, Sam and myself included, these were his most, personal feelings and thoughts on that which, had transpired in Washington D.C. on that day of, January 18th, 1973.

Maj. Coxson, "He was a nice guy that, got tied up with the wrong people" Or, backed the, 'wrong' horse.

On the 8th day of June of that same year, just over off on, the New Jersey side of the Benjamin Franklin Bridge heading north which also, ran into, or intertwined with I-95 and, in a residence just down route 38 from the Cherry Hill Mall where, the champ, Muhammad Ali was said to have once owned a home at that time, Major 'The Maj' Coxson and some members of his family were as it had also been chronicled, and felt through and to, every exact conceivable amount of the emotional, mental and physical gambit conceivable, murdered.

A great number of the details there again, although true, as many of them were also, to a larger extent, they have also been mis-presented, mis-represented, mis-construed and made to be seen as aggravating, acrid or more incendiary to a larger, and varying degree.

Choices. Once again, once a person has choices, or have developed the cognitive processes of knowing in the midst of, understanding desires, wants, needs, the difference between right, wrong and of morality, they then also have, the responsibility or chore of knowing, the consequences or re-actions of things that they mayhap choose to partake of, or participate in.

This is so in the case of, mine's, yours and practically, all of our **lives. Least wise**, that's the way it was, or was meant to be, correct? Major 'The Maj' Coxson although as Sam states it, "was a good man," as I had come to learn, was also one, of those serious gamblers. In addition to that, and the car dealership that he 'owned', just over off the Ben between, **Philadelphia** and **New Jersey**, he made an almost, jocular and failed run for mayor of the city of Camden just on the other side, of the river there again, between, **Philly** and **Camden**.

What I myself, remember most about Major Coxson were, those two famous pictures that, before photo-shop, he was captured in. There was first, that one where, he had the two beauty queens or something-or-the-other contestants sidled up beside each other with him, being sandwiched in between, the two of them. Then, there was that other one with, him standing, in prideful profile in front of the mansion that he, and his family had owned and resided in there, in Cherry Hill.

I am reminded of, a certain scene from, **'The Godfather'** as I think about him, and the car dealership that he owned, or **'ran'** over there, not too far, from his mansion. Cherry Hill itself, was a tough nut around that time, for a man of color to even think of managing, let alone, and to, with a car dealership and a mansion to boot! Also, and a new car dealership, at that!

That was evinced by and in, the champ himself, decision of deciding to, and want to live, there. His car dealership provided a mass number both for, people of color and non-color from both sides of the bridge, with the opportunity to sport around in brand-spanking new Cadillacs. To answer a question that many may as, I'm sure that they have, been plagued by, or have pursued in regard to, Major Coxson and his ability again, around that time, to have been able to do so.

It had been reputed, that Major Coxson was involved with again, an alleged group of Italian men that had been reputed or, had been known to, call themselves, 'The', not, *'Black'* but simply, *'Mafia'*. This would stand to reason why, where and how, the story that, Major Coxson was granted or afforded the opportunity to have been able to, have purchased and maintain the posh life-style that the pictures and news articles, that have been circulated and purported about him, were construed, and came into being again, circulated from.

And there in simply, for Major Coxson, was where his problems initially, and demise had ultimately, resulted from. It was not, that he had gotten on the wrong side with, the again, alleged, *'Black Mafia'* if again, ever, there were one. He had chosen to side with again, the wrong *'Mafia'* again, if ever there were there as well, one which, existed. As for Sam, and what he had to say regarding it. "Brother Beyah, if you would please, because you also know, that people are going to want to know about this, Major Coxson?" *"Well, Major Coxson was a good man. He loved to gamble. He owned a car dealership over there in, Cherry Hill."*

At this, his eyes sort of lit up again, as he turned to me, similar in kind to when, he had been speaking about his sisters, Coretta and Sandra. *"Man, everybody used to go over there and get their Caddys from him! I mean, you could have even gone over there, and got a car from him!"* Again, as he, with that perplexed and astonished look similar in kind to when, he was speaking on his two sisters although this time, with the off-handed, nonchalant and absent-mindedness way that he scratched at his fore-head I then asked him, "Did you get any of your cars from him?"

With a look then, that seemed almost, at the same time both, foreboding and thankful and almost eminently, he responded, *"Nah, I never got one from him."*

The look of foreboding was conjured or wrought up from I believe his, look as if, he had some awareness, fore-knowledge or, spiritual forethought about of or, something not so right with things in that regard, as he again turned, and to make sure that the message was received with certainty and correctly and simply emphasized that with, a resounding and emphatic, unequivocal, not to be questioned-about-it-any further, *"No!"*

In fact, in most of the stories that were relayed to me about, or in regard to, Sam Christian and they entailed his or, the usage or his lack thereof, in that regard of driving skills in doing so, with a vehicle, I've heard the story of a gold Pontiac that he was always said to have been unable, or known to, have attempted to drive. I've also heard from a couple of other reliable sources, Donny Day chiefly among them, and a few of Sam's children to name a few, of his driving skills which, were not very good.

That's a funny picture to think about if you would agree? Something else that. I recently found funny was how most recently that, the standing Pope at present, Pope Francis publicly voiced, his repudiation or conceding in the Vatican's or Papal's awareness of, the existence of one, of the non-existence or, so called, *Mafias*.

Once again, choices. In regard to Major Coxson and what had ultimately transpired there, there was his choice, in the life-style that he had chosen to pursue. Once a person gets to a point in life where awakened at first are, that first realization or awareness of cognizance. There then awakened also, are or is, is that insatiable need for one's fulfillment of one's needs, desires and wants.

Then along with that, then there is, the development of the moral compass that one learns, and carries along with themselves as, they go through life and the fruition of that or those, fulfillments. Once again, as it has already been, is and will, be eluded to and throughout this story, when one is finally, or has ultimately, been endowed with those two very basic or fundamental facets, factors, abilities, wirings or accompaniments in life then, he or she also then, gains or inherits, the responsibility of that which, comes along with, and in regard to those wants, needs or desires of fulfillment.

It was the meeting point, or reckoning of, *'The fitting of the square peg into the round hole'* that comes with such conundrums, or desires en-route to fulfillment. Between what the other, alleged, *Mafia* had to gain and give and, Major Coxson's **wants,** their **available resources** and his **desires,** made for a perfect *fit* that **both** would, and **did**, become profitable from.

And I guess too that, that type of marriage or relationship could lend credence to, the overall consensus of things there, being about, *jealousy* and *greed* between the two alleged, **both, 'Black'** and *'Mafia'*.

But first, given that there, the relationship and dissection of the city between the two factions being likened to that of, the way that people travelling to, and from 9th and Washington having that deeper and more on point poignant understanding or knowing of, the deep-seeded and underlying relationship between the Italians there, and other people from outside of there.

Most of them also, with that understanding also truly knew that too, that was hardly, if at all, the case. True, as it might have been as it has also, been chronicled that, between the two factions, the city had been cut up into a nice neat and profitable pie that everyone was benefitting from. Yes, and as it had also, been written or spoken about in the beginning of how, it would have been at the compass in City Hall where, the city had been cut up, defined and then finally, for a time, divided.

At this point being, Center City is where, a guy by the name of, 'The Center City Hustler' whose real name was, Wisely McNeil was said to have also roamed, with a enough schemes and scams to circulate and fluctuate freely between both factions as well, as the legitimate businesses and politicians there.

At the point heading north from the compass there, everything in that direction going north towards 611 was understood to be, the territory controlled by the faction *allegedly* called, *'The Black Mafia'*. Everything headed south from that point there in Center City was deemed, territory of the other *alleged* faction called just, *'The Mafia'*. In this direction was where, *The Italian Market at 9th & Washington* was situated as, it had been so since, as long, as I could remember, anyways.

Now, heading east towards the river from that point there in City Hall, was pretty much of what, I would call, *'The Guppy Tank'*. Because it was here, and all the way down to the river past Independence Mall where both, of the factions thrived and survived like sharks, on the hapless, sometimes, *'thinking that they are slick'*, searching out or seeking excitement dupes or just plain regular people that mayhap passed through there. And *believe me*, being the City of Brotherly Love that, was a whole lot of, *'Fish'*. *"Fish fit for trimming!"* as, Reggie Cole might have, and more undoubtedly probably did, a time or two, say.

Going west from the compass there, in City Hall was where, the Italian faction co-existed tenuously, pensively and peacefully in accord with the black faction. This was sort of like how, most of the people that traversed through South Philly did, with reverence of the people there, which inhabited it.

In this direction was, West Philly and, as we have already, spoken about there.

None of this mattered to, or played a part in Major Coxson's demise although too, they both did. Now although Sam speaks from the heart, and with a more than modest amount of commiseration for everyone regardless, of the situation as evinced in, the things that he had said, and spoken about in regard to the whole Major Coxson situation, I don't think he was ready for whatever the reason, to truly share about that one, with me.

From several of those intimate sources close to him however, I was able to extract what had really transpired or, had taken place there which, had set that chain and culmination of eventful tragedies into effect. I can say that, with the utmost confidence because, after I had relayed the story as, I had deciphered or, had gotten it, it back to him, that look again, and his physiognomic expression had told me that, I had received it correctly. One of the main things, which kept the cordial and sociable connections or communicative lines open between the two factions was; and that was up until, and after Frank Matthew who, had remained friends with Sam even after, the Tyrone Palmer 'thing' or situation, had transpired, the drugs.

Yes, despite all that good philosophy, and romantic tale of lore given to how, the other faction or so called, the Italian *Mafia* despised and frowned down upon narcotics, still, they were the main suppliers of a large percentage or portion of that, which was poured over and throughout the inter-urban cities and neighborhoods.

'If you wanted cement work done, you called the Italians. If you wanted windows repaired or, something made new on your home, you called the Italians. If you wanted the freshest produce, fish, fruits and vegetables you went down to the 'Italian Market' down around, 9th & Washington.

And if you were a drug dealer, and wanted the best drugs for the cheapest prices again, the top of the food-chain in your connection was, the 'Italians.' And if another human being became such an aggravation or thorn in the side, that you mayhap wanted to see disappear, although the Italian faction again, as it has been noted over time, did and could make such hindrances a memory, when it came to people of color in and around Philadelphia around that time, that was a whole different ball-game.

You see, because when it came to people of color, and especially those, people of color, even the Italians had to call on, and have 'okayed' by someone, to have that particular type of business taken care of. It was necessary. It was a matter of protocol. It had to be that way in order to avoid, 'all-out war' and bedlam in the jungle, which was not, and would not have been beneficial to or, for anyone. And that's where Major Coxson, the gaudy and foppish and very, very brief candidate for the mayoral office of the City of Camden fit the other factions' needs, like, a glove.

With his garish personality and ways, he was considered more, than any of the other things attributed to, or labeled upon him, a facilitator.

So, as the story goes, or went, there were some 'mules', 'made' or,' delivery men', with a shipment of the finest, 'China White', which had been earmarked to be delivered to Camden, that had been intercepted and or, robbed and separated of the product that they were to, deliver before it, or they, had reached, their destination.

Not that the other faction couldn't, or was unable to, take care of the problem themselves. In fact, that was sort of the way that they, were feeling and wanting, to do. But, again, things had changed. It wasn't, and couldn't be done that way anymore at least, for a while.

'The Facilitator'. Being such, this was where, the Major could have ultimately, been either heralded as, a hero or his own executioner given how things could, or that he could turn them out, to be. As they did, it was found, that it was one of those, pretty rough, reckoning and ready-to-do-battle hardened men or 'brothers' from up around, just off the tip of the Black Bottom there nearby, 52nd & Thompson Street, that had done the deed. He was known to, although never known to be, a part of the faction, that allegedly again, began, with its roots up in that apartment building there, in North Philly. To, and with them, he knew his role, and they in turn, respected his although, that was on a precarious ground that both knew, could and would be decimated to, a disfavoring advantage with he, at the losing end of that if, that understanding was broached, encroached or challenged upon. To him, that was of, a minor sort of passing but, foreboding thought that further, emboldened both his, and their resolve and respect for each other.

But one thing was for certain. It was for certain as to, avoid it was as certain as, the biggest war that the City of Philadelphia has at that time, would or could ever see lain fearfully upon it, not happening.

The Italian faction, or those, 'Guineas,' as they called them, weren't for 'certain' going to be coming up into West Philly and look-ing similar of another time going by, and pulling the guy who did it, up and out of there and exacting their revenge or wrath while others again, stood back and looked fearfully, and idly by fearing, the same or loss of the nefarious and high, never-to-be-paid interest rates on the meager six-pence availed, loaned or made possible by, the other faction from down there again by, 9th & Washington. But, something had to be done. Recompense was due.

Again, it was necessary. It was necessary, because otherwise, it would have upset the whole natural order or, equilibrium of things. This was not something that could be just, swept or pushed to the side like, a minor infraction or rule broken or committed by a child. These were, cognitive life decisions. These were, the choices that the players who were participating in that 'Game' or lifestyle, had chosen to make, and or play. They wanted to know, and they wanted him to be made an extreme example of. So, enter the facilitator, Major 'The Maj', 'perfect fit' Coxson. It is here, where, I can empathize to the strongest degree to three things that Sam had said in regard to, Major Coxson, the man himself. "He was a good man," True as it was, that he was a good man, as are most us, but still, in starting out, aren't those, or isn't that the intent of all our decisions, and or, actions?

For him, that goodness was evinced in that which, was shown or given, to his family. In regard to his business savvy, yes, he was good there too. This was so because again, 'is this not, what is expected of any, or most men?' As, he was only doing what he was truly striving to do there, as well. Survive and thrive. Then, also there is, or, as Sam had stated was, one other thing.

That was, that Major Coxson surely must have, 'loved to gamble!' or, was in love with the hustle of it. Because, and pardon another pun, he was now, like never before, playing with some, 'Major' stakes at wager here where, odds given, what was riding on his great calculation skills of what he might suggest be done to appease, placate and please to satisfaction, every one too, with their shares or things, at stake here.

Minute and or as selfish, as one may think, that to be in the small context, in regard to the 'big picture', it was also still too, as explained and was re-iterated, important to, and for the 'Major' to keep in the equation or, mind.

Then finally again, as Sam had also stated, something that I am strongly inclined to agree with. And that was, ***"He was a good man that, just got caught up in a bad situation or, way."*** It had to be done. It was one of those cardinal 'things' or violations, there-of. It was a must. That's how, things were done for such infractions or transgressions. That was a one, of the precepts that all including, they themselves, the ***'Black'*** faction or, ***'Mafia'*** had to, and did build, their own foundations on, and abide by. Again, at leastwise, that's how it was, initially. But, also again, one thing was for certain again though. Since, and because of that, they or, that other faction of alleged, ***'Mafia'*** were not, and wouldn't be the ones allowed that, were going to do it. Things just weren't anymore, and never again, would be done that way. At least wise, not in regard to, or with regard to, the alleged, ***'Black'*** faction or, ***'Mafia'***.

Again, in a nice and neat paradox little world or, place where, if there really existed, such a thing as a, *'Mafia'* or faction capable, of committing such acts as that, which had to be done.

So, the contract had been put out. Two-hundred thousand dollars had been offered as, the bounty for the person or persons who had pulled off, or had taken the South (down there by, 9th & Washington Avenue) Philadelphia faction's product.

It was probably, as we will never truly know, Major, 'The Maj', Coxson who had thought of the idea or, way out, of the situation for everyone involved. It was probably again, as we will also, never truly know, 'The Maj' or, Major that brought, the idea to the aggrieved or, injured faction as well.

It was for certain, as we do truly know, Major Coxson that had brought the idea or solution to the faction that would be, taking charge of the chore or, 'deed'. It would have been considering, the 'business' that they were all involved in, an equitable thing or course, of recompense had everyone stuck to the script probably again, set out and prescribed by, 'The Maj'.

Again, had they. But, as history and the journals have provided and evinced, that was not going to be so. The 9th & Washington faction, had other ideas. They were indeed or, going to have or, have exacted, their revenge, compensation or resolve for the infraction. They were going to do it, in the same time worn manner that had worked, and been the trade mark of themselves since, their 'own' or, again, **alleged** inception. It would be done so that, all knew, and would again know, that time-worn knowledge which was that, 'you don't mess with the alleged, *Mafia*, its money, its drugs or any, of its operations'. **Again,** had there in fact, been an alleged, *'Mafia'* of any sort.

Then, as an extra added 'public' benefit, they would also too, as may have been their plans again, no one will ever truly know, to, in the process, make 'fools' or shine light on the foolishness or ineptness of the other faction or, alleged, *'Black Mafia'*.

So, after the contract was fulfilled, they accomplished and did all this by simply, doing and again, pardon the pun, one 'major' yet small, minute thing.

They just simply, after the deed was done, walked away sort of like, the deal with Sam and Frank Matthews without payment or, any semblance of recompense for, services rendered. This in turn, simply, sealed the fate for, Major 'The Maj' Coxson.

All the rest including, the now permanent wedge that was set between the two factions were as, I am certain that, you have already surmised, or know is, simply just, his story meaning, the other guy's.

'Didn't I Blow Your Mind This Time, Didn't I?' "Harlem, that's 'Uptown' baby!" October the twenty-fourth, nine-teen hundred and seventy-one. As it had been chronicled, a robbery had taken place in, Harlem New York. Usually, although still wrong as it was, and maybe, a robbery especially in such a city as New York, was really, no big 'to-do' about. And even now as, that is still my contention except, in regard to the character ,or say like, the individual that I am writing about, Sam Christian.

This is so, because one, as a result of our collaborative efforts in, what is his, and now, our story. Then, there's two, a great number of things from the courts of the land to, those being, the 'general public' in conjunction with i.e., the news (television & radio), newspapers and the common rumor or, gossip mills aside from, the judicial courts in having their say, did not really know, what lay behind the reasons for this particular robbery taking place in, the first place.

And too, I'm sure, that was mainly so, for all those number of years, because of the air, and mystique and possibly, out of fear for any of the possible things that many may have feared of, the retributive things that could happen, if things relating to, or in regard to again, this alleged, **'Black Mafia'** were delved upon or, into too, deeply.

This in turn had first, gave cause or, laid the foundation for the harboring, bolstering and even still to this day, perpetuation and exacerbation of the destructive, self-serving and self-destructive attitudes, behaviors and mentalities that plague and threaten to all but systematically, dissipate and extinguish the population of our, urban and diverse cultures of commune or, 'ities'.

Now, although this type of attitude or mentality had existed and was something that was in effect long before either the likes of, Sam Christian or the so called, or alleged, *'Black Mafia'*, in regard to once again, the alleged, *'Black Mafia'* and Philadelphia, those attitudes, and mentalities have again, and still to this day, been the main vehicle or mind-set that most assuredly seems, the path or route leading to, that destruction.

Because of this type of thinking, the only point of view, which always seemingly endeavors to, shine the most negative, demeaning and oft-times, correct light on such situations, and people are received in the urban communities with that, just as oft-times, incorrect sense of reverence and revelry to be praised, and ascribed for.

However, in a further attempt to demonize and make a situation or person seem that much more, abhorrent or reprehensible and seemingly deserving, of the oft-times disparaging, and harsh forms of justice and public ridicule that are again, more than oft-times, meted out, law-enforcement and the judicial system as well as, the media just as oft-times, leaves out or, keeps certain aspects from the public that mayhap shed a different or, more pragmatic and palpable or, capable of being digested receptive reason or, reasons for some of the things that may have or, may had perchance happened.

And these actions in turn, just as oft-times, has or, does assists and bolsters or exacerbates that mentality that mayhap possibly lead to, that destruction of the urban family unit and its communities.

And so as promised, in leaving no stone 'un-turned' in regard to this particular individual, Sam Christian, we will present a side in regard to what had transpired in Harlem on October 24th, 1971 that has never really been delved into or, spoken upon, about in or again, through any of the regular sources of information, those being, the news media, law-enforcement, judicial system or, by you, the astute, assuming and thirsty for now, in regard to this particular individual, knowledgeable public. Although, I had spoken in regard to a number of the ways and the things that Jeremiah Shabazz, (Pugh) mayhap have assisted in the down-fall or restructuring of, the, 'Top of The Clock in a light or, way that had taken some time, and a great amount of work to re-build, I had purposely, for the sake of hoping one would, get a full and clear picture of things, left out a number of the other things that he, or they had done as, it fit perfectly, into what I am about to expound on at, this point or juncture.

No, the selling of papers (Muhammad Speaks) and mentally, and spiritually trying to uplift a people, was not the only thing that the Nation of Islam or, the, 'Top of The Clock' were attempting to do. That empowerment, was not just about words.

It went well beyond, that. Although, I cannot fully or, with clarity (for, the story or, at least, this one, would never end) speak on the 'how', in regard to other cities outside of Philadelphia, because of my fortune in again, having this blessed opportunity and, the informational resources availed to me courtesy, of the subject, I can give example of some of those ways, things and 'how's' there, in Philadelphia.

Despite what any of the incongruent advocates have to say, Philadelphia was a city desiring, and because of the, 'Top of the Clock' striving physically, to become self-sufficient for the people of color there. They had their own bakeries. And as it had although, with a certain amount of almost despise and venom been stated, they built a school as well as, a child care center. Many could remember as I'm sure, the juice (literally) that was sold. Then there was also too, as many may recall as well, when, the unions down at the Food Center attempted to hinder or, put a stop to the unloading of the ships full of fish that they, the Nation of Islam had transported in by refusing, and commanding their workers to, not unload them. That must have been a sight or, something hard for the union to swallow as, the Nation of Islam or, more poignantly, Jeremiah then, contracted on their own, the ships to go where, the fish was caught and kept and first loaded onto the ships, and then with their own workers (Brothers of the Nation of Islam), unloaded those same ships down at the Food Center there, in South Philly.

They held interests or, molded in a large, roundabout way in, the entertainment or, music business that was there, also. On my own accord, opinion and volition I think that, this is something that both, Mr. Kenneth Gamble and, Mr. Leon Huff of, Gamble & Huff Entertainment could concur with. Then also, there was, 'Philly Groove Records'.

With the assistance of, Eugene (Bo) or, (Abu Bakar) Baynes and under the guidance of, Stan Watson and Sam Bell, Philly Groove Records had become at that time, successful and observed, a legitimate competitor or, adversarial and competing to reign in, the ears of listeners to again, said, Gamble & Huff Entertainment and was responsible for such acts as, The Delfonics and the female group, First Choice before folding as, Arista Records then came on the scene, bought, and then shelved, the whole concept and company.

'**Payola**', was not the only obstacle that, many artists and their respective labels had to contend with, back during those times just as, still exists now even, to date.

Also rampant, was the 'real' and literal problem of, getting paid for many of them, as well. This problem, as one may be aware of today, has been remedied by both, many of the artists and their labels demanding payment upfront before any actual exchanges, events or performances take place and then too as, many of them, just created their own companies or labels although, that didn't or, doesn't always pan out in the way that, they might or mayhap be, endeavoring for. But, mostly, this is because of, not the greatest business savvy and or, foolish spending.

Unfortunately again, starting out, this wasn't always the case, and as, many of the artists could and can attest to, and their labels, many were, and often are, 'stiffed' or, 'clipped' out of what was or, may be due to them. Although this was not always the case or, what was needed by many, but when things like this took place, those to, which whom or, it had happened to have been visited upon or to, were glad for such people as the likes of say, a, Sam Christian. In this case, of what had transpired in Harlem in a nut shell although, not brought to the light, in that instance or trial, this was exactly, the case.

Yes, it was called and, in most other instances, it might have been a robbery.

However, in and on, my take on this particular instance, I had surmised, observed, or had found that, a little bit difficult to swallow given that, as they arrived there to 'rob' the store, not too far and practically, lying in wait was, the police or, police officer. As it turned out, somebody, one or, people were owed some funds for services rendered or products delivered that, they did not receive recompense, for.

Sorry if, once again, the culmination of this part of the story as well, did not meet one's expectations of something dramatic or, extremely or, overly exciting in regard once again to, Sam did not come to fruition or, pan out again, here.

However, on a footnote, there was a thing that took place there on that date that, one may find calls for, the slight raising of an eyebrow in interest or that, one may also call, slightly intriguing. This was in regard to what had transpired there during the robbery that one could say, left Sam in the position where, he had no other choice, or option than to, fire upon or, back at that police officer or anyone else, that would have entered the record store in the first place on that date.

And, the really interesting or, intriguing part at least to me, was where I, in my own mind, had deduced how, it played a major or semi-major part in what had transpired in Washington D.C. on that date of, January 18th, 1973.

As it had been relayed to me from yet again, another or, one of those same reliable sources, "If a 'certain individual' did not pull off and leave Sam that day, I believe, Sam would not have been jammed up in there, that day." Since, this is really not a story about name dropping, but Sam Christian, I have chosen for the sake of, 'Just Because' to every now and again, leave certain names out as I felt or, feel it necessary as, putting them in would serve no other purpose than to well, let's just say that, to name them or put them in at certain degrees or points would not really make a difference to this man's story one way or, the other. I am as promised, still giving you're the story in its entirety, in regard to, Sam Christian.

Still, I will leave you to your own devices and gratification to the extent of your own satisfaction, thrills, inquisitive minds or whatever to, fill in those certain, thirsted desires or blanks or, 'names' where you may choose or, see fit.

However also, if along the way, you should in your desires or thirst, connect certain dots and come up with what may be a correct guess as to who, turned out to be who or, 'what was what' in such certain or, any of the given circumstances then, 'Bully', for you!

Because once again, it matters not still, in regard to this man, and this story about him because, in the conclusion, everything still, 'is what it is' or, was. Now, with all that being stated, the same individual whom, just might have been able to had afforded Sam the opportunity to not, have had to exchange gunfire and ultimately hit, that same police officer in the process as he still, though barely for the time being, somehow, made it out of that record store and Harlem, was the same individual that when, I asked Sam about the situation that took place in Washington D.C. on, January 18, 1973, Sam stated, *"It was the work of either, an insane or, scared man."*

In addition to that, it was also the same individual that, with whom he, that individual, and his cohort that I wrote about earlier, that may have had or, hatched a certain nefarious plan or plot that was designed to cause the demise of Donny Day before, Sam's interceding, interception or, 'Stepping in' once again, those, few years later.

For all the things that Sam might have been, could have been, and or, had been alleged to have been he was, if nothing else, and above all else, loyal to, whatever the cause that he, had been on.

Again, he was the quintessential definition and model of, a 'soldier' or, of what one would assume or, presume the image of, a soldier to be. This fact too, was evinced in the way that he, had let that same individual that had, by all the standards set by the streets, tried, and almost succeeded in the worst of ways whether, consciously or, subconsciously to screw him over twice, not only to live, but to thrive while doing so, as well. And this, he did simply, and diligently for the sake and fact that, they were bound mainly, by their religion that they both, had chosen to practice ardently and earnestly, with spirit.

There was the time when Sam was once overheard to have said to Jeremiah, "Hold on to that position! Because, if you ever lose it, I'm going to kill you!" Sam, was present while this particular story, was being relayed to me, and to which, he did not offer up a rebuttal or denial to it, as it was being relayed. I add this now, to again further, evince how dedicated, and loyal he was to his religion, and the charges of same, set before him in his obeisance with regard to, the tenants of it. He had made this statement after Jeremiah had committed what one mayhap could consider or, could be considered, the vilest of transgressions against a fellow member short of just literally, killing him. But yet still, he held on, and respected to the highest, Jeremiah's position as their leader, all the way up to, and ultimately through until he, was removed from it, by the son of the Honorable Elijah Muhammad, Imam Wallace Dean Muhammad who, had taken hold of the helm and began transitioning the brotherhood in the direction of what was now again, as stated previously, being realized, and accepted as, the 'True Religion' of Islam in America, the Sunni religion.

BARRY D. WADE

'Samuel Richard Carter'

It was after that, the Harlem Record store incident that, soon to be, F.B.I's most wanted list number, 321 became to many, the nefarious golem or malevolent apparition that one did not really want to see or, be visited upon for the fear of, breathing one's last breath. Although and in large part to a major extent, true, that was also when Sam, who had earlier before that incident in Harlem had, skipped out on a million dollar bail for another incident in Philly really, went on the 'fly' as they, in Philly had called it, 'taking flight to avoid prosecution'. That incident, which had taken place in Philly where, Sam had skipped out on that million dollar bail was also, in large part, because of Sam and others there, that had done likewise, was why and how, getting bailed out of jail in Philly after an incident, had been totally re-arranged, and changed the bail bonds system or, what one had to go through to get bail there, in the Pennsylvania and Philadelphia legal systems.

'Call to Duty'

A number of things took place during that time, which had, turned up the heat or put pressure on, not only Sam and the alleged, **Black Mafia**, but the Black Muslim community, as a whole.

There was for starters, the storming by the police officers of the City of New York of the Harlem mosque on April 14, 1972 in which, one of the police officers, Phillip Cardillo lost his life. When that had taken place, and there, at the mosque were, meetings on what should be done to combat the situation, there, in attendance too, was Sam undetected by any, but a rare few, that he wanted to know, he was there, in full disguise. Again, *'Everywhere, but 'nowhere' '*.

Then, there was the Vietnam 'Police Action', which, was winding down to a close.

In that, there was the mass number of veterans of the conflict who, were returning to America and addicted to the drugs that, had followed them home, and which, was flooding the streets. There, in addition to their returning back without even, a modest amount of fanfare yet, a great amount of anger and confusion of why, they had been there in the first place was, the lack of 'real' support from government officials, which they most certainly needed to recover, from the horrors of that atrocity. At home, in addition to the opposition and dissension of that conflict there was still, as it had been before that conflict, the dissension and opposition to pretty much everything that had anything to do, with the government and the way that it had been going about, in doing the things that it did. From the government standpoint, something had to be done to reign in control of the things that were spiraling insanely off the axis of the norm what with, the other protests and things, that had reached their boiling point which also, had nothing in the least, to do with the Nation of Islam itself still yet, with and in regard for, the fight for equal rights. They, the Nation of Islam were but, a small, but yet still, major part of the problem.

In regard to the storming of the Harlem mosque, not only did it become, a very mired and murky game of, not exactly who, was at fault and whose rights were violated. But also, it had become a tense and not really, ever to be settled stalemate or, 'impasse'. The things that had taken place there, had left things deeper still, and further, between many of the police and the 'Offices' of 'Law-Enforcement' and the Nation of Islam at a pretty much, deeper than, the previous 'deeper still' and still, heated stand-still that would have to be figured out elsewhere, other than in, the racially divided city that New York was, and as many may still feel, is now, at that time. But it still, left a bitter taste in the minds, and mouths of 'the powers that be' or were, at that time, which made things doubly hard, for many people of color which again, had nothing to do with, that whole situation.

So when, what had happened in Washington D.C. did, one could say that, there and then, was when a can of troubles or candle was lit or opened that, was most definitely, not needed or feasible, to the overall cause.

When that had happened, both the public, and 'the powers that be' or, were at that time, became emotionally and instantaneously en- and 'out'- raged. And that is when things, had again, pretty much began to crumble and fall apart for the 'Top of the Clock' and or, the alleged, *'Black Mafia'* as more, of a negative light was shed upon things there, that really weren't needed or congruent in regard to, the bigger scheme of things. And where, was Sam?

Sam had been mainly, in Detroit where, in addition to travelling back and forth between there, and Philly as it had also been stated to me, by others, and he himself, serving, the Nation as he had begun and done so in his early days in Philly, before the tales, lure, legends, lies, truths and the other things spoken, written about once again, the alleged, *'Black Mafia'* and all the other stuff that had been attributed to, or, of what had been alleged or again, of the things that they, or he, had actually, done.

And the funny thing about that, as I had come to learn while researching and gathering material for this story was, the same appeal and positive or fabled heroic attributions that he had garnered or was legend to have been in his city of birth, Philly, even before and still even, after the alleged, *'Black Mafia'* thing, one could, double or even without doubt, triple that, and still not reach an inkling or miniscule of the person or, persona that he was said to have been, or had become to meant, to many of the people there, in Detroit.

"Man, those cops in Buffalo are so mean that, 'they would kill a dead man'!"

"Hey, this is him! This is that guy! This is the one that we have been searching for."

It was a detective in Buffalo New York who, had figured it out.

Well, to say 'figured', would not exactly be, or quite the term to, use. Although indeed, they had an active and on-going search in effect for Sam, they had not been quite fortunate in that search.

And, it was not that, they had given up on that search in as much as, the leads had grown pretty cold. It had long ago, as well as, from the beginning, become an exasperating and tiresome search.

And besides that, it was not as if suddenly, crime had come to stop elsewhere, within the union or confines of, the United States. That was especially so, in the black community. So, although the search was active, and they really wanted badly, to catch up to Sam and in fact, quite badly, it was not so much as, with that initial great sense of urgency as it had been from the beginning.

That was, and is the thing, with law-enforcement. 'They could afford to wait'. They could even, afford to, 'make mistakes or, a mistake here and there. That was because, they were granted by 'providential', virtue of their job with the multiple opportunities to get it right. Now, as you may already know, on the flipside, if you were or, just happened to be someone or, that someone whom, law-enforcement was in search of or, for whatever the reason, you knew that, you only had one opportunity at being caught unless, as evinced from the Philadelphia thing with Sam Christian and others, those other, special 'rare' and, few.'

And, it wasn't as if, this particular detective, had been assigned to the case or task force assigned particularly, to track him, Sam, down either. He had just been in the office one day, reading one of those, 'True Detective' magazines. You probably or may, remember the ones. These were the ones, that had come out long before, 'America's Most Wanted' or any of those other so-called, 'Police' or 'reality' crime shows that let one, the viewer or critic be, the junior detective or, assistant to law-enforcement in tracking down said, fugitives or criminals.

And that's basically, and the 'un-dramatic' truth on how, they had found out about or, of Sam's whereabouts, and location.

They had also found, as of late, that he had been mainly frequent-ing, the Detroit area.

The best set-up in the world.

I know and remember earlier that, I had wrote some things that to many, may seem, very disparaging in regard to, Jeremiah Shabazz and the damage that he, in particularly, had caused to, 'The Top of The Clock' and the black Muslim community as a whole. I am also aware that, there are many out there that may find, or may seemingly be, of the mind-set or fall into agreement that many, of those things men-tioned earlier were, dead-on true, and in exact with regard to, those things mentioned. However still, be that as it may either way, as, they were just my, and mine's alone, personal observations and perceptions on first, the things that had taken place and then, the final outcome of how things ultimately, turned out to be there, in regard to Philly.

So, in all fairness, and for the sake of integrity, it is my hope that one, not negate or let become askew, the great number of other posi-tive things that he, and they, had also done to the good and, for the benefit of the city, and a great number of the blacks and other people of color, there. Many of them, have went on, and still to this day, con-tinue to great things. Not only have and are many of those things that were done, were done for, and in the city by many of those faithful and recipients there, but many of those positive things that were done and continue to be done, were done throughout, the world as well. And too, just a minor passing thought, it could have just been quite, the smallest bit possible that, in regard to the things or, activities that had taken place within and because of, 'certain' people at the, 'Top of the Clock' that, what had transpired might not be exactly, the picture that many of the public and others had made it out to be. I don't know, it's possible. In that, I mean, let's say for instant, you have a great boss or, supervisor under whose, command or employ that one, or many, may be working for. Now, let's say that they, under the command are miscreants or, screw ups. Who, do you think, that the blame or whatever is going to fall on when things, go haywire or, awry? I mean again, I don't know, but it's possible. No, you don't think so?

Anyhow or, ways, with that being stated, and in regard to this particular juncture here in his, and his relationship with Sam, I am now again, going to elaborate and expound on one other or, not so noble, or noteworthy thing that had transpired while yet, keeping in mind, in addition to, those other noble and noteworthy positive accounts and things noted in, and regarding himself.

And still again, and as, it has been relayed to me from one of those, in Sam's most closest and intimate circles of people or close associates, and for me, one of those reliable, and valuable sources about, and in regard to again, Jeremiah.

I am, and have had the fortunate and blessed opportunity of giving it to you from, a pretty accurate and honest perspective as well because, of that. I state all of that, to simply state to anyone that, and mayhap more than likely feel or, have either for, or against any of the things written in regard to him, and with regard to him, and Sam construed as either, condescending or otherwise, disparaging.

It however, and above all else, still is, 'what it was!' to the plus or, negative for either, condescension or disparagement and with that, a moot point as well or, too, the truth.

It had been stated that, towards the end or, after things had begun to really plume, blow up or, spiral out of control for, 'The Top of The Clock', that Jeremiah, as it had started becoming, to be wondered about and ultimately believed, amongst a certain few, became, a 'C.I'. or, confidential informant for the federal government that was now, hot on, and dogging his, and 'The Top of The Clock's' every move.

Now, whether or not, that, this assertion or unfounded accusation was, were or mayhap been true, I like you, may never know. But, given what had transpired after that detective in Buffalo had stumbled or, happened upon

Sam's picture in that magazine which gave rise and them, the scent again and turned up the heat again for Sam, one could, or would say that, it seems or seemed, awfully peculiar and the slightest bit plausible.

Then to, add to credence, to the suspicion or, head-scratching was, what Jeremiah then again, as it had been alleged from that particular and reliable source that, had relayed this part of the story to me, had asked Sam to do, next.

Mind you, the reader once again that, while these conversations are taking place between the party and myself, Sam is sitting right there amongst us, quietly listening.

There is a footnote here, of which, I am urgently compelled right and now, in regard to this source that brought this thought and part of the story to, my mind. This individual, that had relayed this part of the story to me, as it had been in later years stated, and circulated amongst a vast and large number of the members and brothers of the Philadelphia Muslim community was, one of those individuals elected to practically, the highest position short that of imam with-in the community bestowed, with the opportunity or show of eminence to have staved off or, had prevented, the ultimate all-out war where, a large number of brothers both of, and outside of the community or, brotherhood had lost their lives in the so called, 'turf' and 'policies' war that had come, or had followed as a result of, the drugs that had once again, over-shadowed and eclipsed that cause (self-independence & government to abstain and refrain from) and then finally, attain that, that they had initially from the beginning, set or, sought out, to achieve. So again, none of us, are above blame. Just stating, the obvious, the truth and an assured perception.

One thing, that one also, could be assured and certain of. In fact, they could be as certain of this as, you could be as curtained, of the sun by God's will rose and rises each, morning.

That was, that Sam never, ever, travelled anywhere without, his guns. Wait, I'm wrong. There was one place that, he did not take them. The only place that he did not travel with them was, as just the same as anyone else maybe and hopefully, and that was, inside of the mosques or masjids where, he worshipped, and served. And even there, rest assure that, they were close, very close!

But other than that, if you saw Sam, you knew he had his guns, and on him! Jeremiah had told him, Sam on this particular occasion that, he had needed him to make an un-scheduled and 'on the fly' trip back to Detroit. He then made, that odd and 'out of character', request or imploration.

He then told or, urgently requested that, he meaning Sam, leave his guns behind back in Philly, as he had done so,(made the trip to Detroit). That part was true, as I later inquired of Sam, and he had confirmed that in fact, yes, Jerimiah had relayed or implored of him, this particularly, 'odd' request to, the individual that had brought his thoughts and this, to my attention.

It was then, and during a layover in New York when, the detective that had stumbled upon, and the police force of the city of, Albany and the State of New York and all of its, Judicial and Law-Enforcement batteries first apprehended and then, thoroughly, trounced upon, and then afterwards, thoroughly and physically thrashed, Federal Bureau of Investigations Most Wanted Fugitive number, three-twenty-one or, three-two-one forcing him into, a realization and observation of the possibility that, *"Man, those cops in Albany are so mean that, they would kill a dead man!"* At that exact time in which, that incident or capturing had taken place, Federal Bureau of Investigations Most Wanted Fugitive number three-twenty-one, three, and two and one or, Samuel Richard 'Carter' born, Samuel Richard Christian, had been on that list, for a total of five days however, one may want to, chalk that up to fate, luck, misfortune, friend or brother, at that time of his, apprehension.

He had made that list on, December 7th, 1973 a day which, thirty-one years earlier, as Franklin Delano Roosevelt had lamented, and Sam would no doubt from that time on, or shortly there-after like about, those five days later in 1973, agree with that, *"would live in infamy!"*

On the 12 day of that month, after the physical, before the court and physical reprisals had been reprised those several or so times over again, and again on him, and in the interim before that date, he was promptly taken off, to await his day in court with his capture, he had been on that list a total of, count them, *five days!* In addition to any of the other things that, this brief period might or, may have meant, there was one other thing that stood out paramount above all of those other 'might's' or, 'maybes' and that was, they had, as evinced in that whole little short episode or expand of those five days wanted, and very badly, Sam!

That 'not-so-much-with-a-sense-of-major-urgency' or almost, 'laissez-faire' existence went swiftly out the 'window' and, was expeditiously dissipated to the 'winds' in that, five-day time span of them 'catching a scent' of, and then finally, to the point in time of him, being transported to a less brutal and safer for him, confines.

As he is relaying this part of the story to me, there is a look etched upon his face of a very clear, and lucid memory of just how bad, that thrashing was. It was neither, a practiced look nor, was it one of a sudden and vivid memory or reminder. Rather, what it seemed was, one imprinted upon him for eternity upon the initial point when he, had again initially, went through it.

It was at this point where, he had elaborated or went into the reason or, reasons for his ever, and eternal for him, of having had been compelled towards this thought as he stated, *"Man, they had beat me so bad, that I was trying to play or act, like I was dead! And they still, kept beating me!"* That was a time when, in somewhat similar to now, when it seemed, and seems pretty much, not that big of a deal or lost to, kill a person of different ethnicity which, had just happened to have been, and especially at that time, black or 'colored', men.

But, there was a problem when it came to Sam because, as you may have come to surmise or see about him at that time, he was and had gotten to be, and not just in Philly any more as I have previously stated, a pretty big deal. And it would have caused somewhat of, an uproar or riot if by, or perhaps any chance that, they would have caused his sudden and abrupt demise. This was especially so too, because one, had it been done so, they would have had to answer those questions about, 'why' and 'how' this was done and 'him' without, the benefit or further proof of the monster that he had been cast to be, his guns. Then, there was, the always ever present and could not be denied or shunned, number two.

Two, would have been, many and, many more of having to answer a further question of like say, 'How could this happen if,' if per say, 'All things on one side or end, had been done, or had gone exactly or, as strictly as 'planned' '?

But again, without regard to any of those theories, as he had stated directly, and unequivocally to, moi', me, myself, 'they had taken him as pretty far, and as close as, **'one, could get without actually, succeeding.'**

Now, as to why, I have opted to call this chapter, **'The best set-up in the world!'**

The reason is, because again, as I have spoken or written those disparaging things in regard to my observations and perceptions and that one other disparaging thing, or rumor given, what they were doing and supposed to be about, there is again, one thought that I myself, can and could not let become askew or negated.

And that thought in my mind, stood and still stands solid against, and capable of, on an even firmer foundation of being paramount above even, if that most sacrilegious sin given, again, what they were supposed to be, or actually involved in were, true. Because for whatever the reason, nefarious or wholly sanctified, if Jeremiah had not done or requested what he did or had been alleged to have said or done, this story that I am relaying now, and given the curious the opportunity to indulge in, would not be taking place. And for that, regardless of how one may perchance have concluded, or decided to feel, for this preservation perspective and important part of some serious history in that, it need not or, let be strewn and scattered by the wayside like litter or dust to the wind, we owe Jeremiah, a very great debt of gratitude for, the, *'Best Set-up in the World!'*. He, by requesting or doing, what was alleged of him if, that truly were the case, had set Sam up so that, he did not have to die that day which, those law-enforcement officials in Albany would have surely loved, for that opportunity to have, killed him.

And then, where would that, have left us, to feed that insatiable appetite and need to find enjoyment in someone else's trials, tribulations, predicaments and drama?

'No Commandos or Killers scaling down from the ceiling'

If not stated before, I once asked Sam why he used the name, 'Carter' as his alias. Not that I was expecting anything dramatic or something 'slick and fly' that would congeal and go right along with the life, or persona that had become associated with his, becoming. But nor, did or would I have expected the answer that he did give me either. His plain and simple reason for using this alias was simply because, his mother who, was a fond supporter and admirer of one, James Earl Carter Jr. The rest of us, may know him as, the 39th president of The United States and a member of the Democratic Party and also, one of the greatest humanitarians in the world that had ever lived, Jimmy Carter. That was it, the whole 'ball of wax', 'in a nut shell' reason. Considering, the individual and the serious nature of the things associated with him, and the serious importance of this book, I just found that little bit' or, piece of information a tad amusing, which compels me to every now and again smile, "Because my mother always liked, Jimmy Carter." While I am digressing for a moment, there was one other thing that always seems to make me smile in amusement after having the opportunity, which I have had in sitting down and getting from his mouth, the story of, Sam Christian.

And that was the story of when, he had 'happened upon' one of, the fair amount of soon-to-be mothers of one of his soon to be also, many children. Here it was, big and bad Sam Christian had been sent on a mission of mercy to save from the streets and its life, one wayward and insolent girl.

As he was telling me that story, I was pretty certain and set in my mind that, the issue of someone standing in the way or, stopping him from what he had been sent to do, was the furthest thing from his mind as he added while patting, his left hip when I asked, "Were you worried about anybody stopping you?", *"No, because I had a couple of partners by my side."*

Still though, in addition to the friends that he had with him on his, left hip, he had with him, one of his brothers whose name was, Zaid. Zaid's government or parental given name was, Alvin Sapp. Zaid, was and had proven himself well in the beginning of the, 'First Resurrection' to be one of those, most faithful brothers. If any, have ever saw that 'famous' picture that, had adorned the Daily News Paper that one day there, in Philly, they would have seen Brother Zaid there with, Jerimiah and several of the other brothers of, 'The Top of The Clock'. He was, the second brother from the left, there. His faith, was so strong that, when he had gotten word of the turf wars that were going on with-in the brotherhood and behind the thing that, they had sought to eliminate brought actual, anguished tears to his eyes. That was pretty much where, and when, the thing that they had fought so hard to achieve, was taken out of Zaid.

Anyways, now here it was, Sam and the young lady going back and forth. Sam, *"Come on down from there!"* The future mother of one of his children, "No!" Sam, *"You better come on down from there!*

Your grandmother sent me to, come get you! Now, come on down from there and let's go!" Her once again, "No!" She had been danc-ing as I wrote earlier, at one of the bars over there on, the 'Strip' or, 52nd Street. *"You better come on down from there before, I come up there and bring you down myself!"* Still again, without an ounce less of defiance, "No!" As he is telling me this, and at this part, I can still envision and see upon his face as, if it had just happened yesterday, the look of, stupefied astonishment at his perplexity of what to do because it had seemed to him that, he had caught a 'Fire Cracker' in this young lady who seemingly, didn't care about or, who, he was as she still, did not come down as he had commanded, from off of the stage.

This was Sam Christian and he had, by her, been put in a posi-tion of having to do something since, his persona and command did not produce any results. There were people present, and at stake was the fact that, if he had not gotten her to come down off of that stage, people although still in total fear and reverence as they would be of him, would have that one little thing that they would always be able to secretly, laugh or giggle about in regard to him. For probably, one of the first times in his life, Sam had been trapped in a situation for what, he did not know, what to do about and it had him sweating. She was not, and did not have any intentions of following his, orders.

He had to do something. So, what did he do? *"Zaid, go on up there, and get that girl down from there."* And that's how he en-countered, the mother of one, of his children as she kicking, and scratching was brought down from the stage and eventually, back to her grandmother by Zaid, and he. Of course, we know the rest of that story as, the grandmother later lamented, "I sent you to go and get my granddaughter, and you really went a got her alright!"

Many of you might recall, a certain writer that went by the name of, Thomas Kennerly Wolfe. Not to be confused with, the other great writer, Thomas Clayton Wolfe who, had penned such great works as, 'You Can't Go Home Again' and 'Look Homeward Angel'. Thomas

Clayton Wolfe on the one hand, was born on the date of, October the 3rd, 1900 in Asheville North Carolina. He died on, September the 15th, 1938. The story of his life too, in itself, is a fascinating one that briefly, and arduously passed in a sad way, through New York City if one should perchance, get the opportunity to read up on, or about him.

Thomas Kennelly Wolfe or, 'Tom' Wolfe on the other hand as he, is more famously, and familiarly known, was born on March the 2nd, 1931. As of this writing, he is not deceased. He, was born in Richmond Virginia. Other than, the close proximity between Asheville and Richmond, and having the same names, there is no biological or genealogical relationship between, the two.

Tom Wolfe, is responsible for such great works as, 'The Electric Kool-Aid Acid Test', 'The Right Stuff' and, 'The Bonfire of The Vanities' amongst, a host of many others. Chronicled and considered, somewhat of a hell-raiser in his own right as evinced by, a number of noted spats that were very well chronicled, in newspaper and magazine articles with a few other notable authors, he too also, a time or two, blazed or made a path through a few of the boroughs in New York City. In his book, 'The Bonfire of The Vanities' in the foreword and dedication section, he made a very special dedication to two other notable, New York figures. One was, Attorney, Edward Walter Hayes. Edward or, 'Eddie' as he, as of this writing, is more familiarly known, in addition to being the model for the character, 'Tommy Killian' in Tom's book was also responsible, for the settling of the estate of one, Andy Warhol, a famous photographer and artist in his own right that I'm quite certain that, many have indeed, have heard of. In addition to that, he has also been noted as, representing several organized crime figures, in some major crime cases, in the New York Court Systems. "Doffing his hat," about Eddie, he wrote in his book, 'who, walked among the flames, pointing at the lurid lights.' About the other figure, it was written, "And he wishes to express his deepest appreciation to, Burton Roberts who first, showed the way." In addition to being one of the inspirations for one of the characters in Tom's, 'Bonfire of The Vanities', Justice Burton Roberts, was the presiding judge over Sam's case for his attempted murder trial in New York. That was the charge that, he, Sam had been charged with being that, the officer did not die when he had exchanged gun-fire with Sam.

According to Sam, he, Justice Burton Roberts was a fair-minded judge who, accepted no histrionics in his courtroom. It was also he, who had made statement about there being, 'no, 'commandos or killers' scaling down from the ceiling' thus, allowing, in the interim during the breaks in deliberations, Sam the opportunity to sit down in the courtroom with his family and other members.

Again, it was he, who had made the statement, "I'm not going to let you, the prosecution stand in my courtroom and paint a picture of, Al Capone and nor, am I going to let the defense sit in here and paint a picture of, Robin Hood either."

On several occasions during the trial and again, in between deliberations, he even allowed Sam, the opportunity to sit and have lunch with those same, family members and other associates who mayhap have, been in attendance during, those certain days. Justice Roberts, also, had a brother that too, was a judge in the, New York Court Systems. His name was, George Roberts and according to Sam, he was like, *"night and day"* in comparison with, his brother. However, as told to me by Sam, Justice Burton being the elder of the two, and on a higher court than George, never overruled, on a case that his brother may have, presided over. A fair and compassionate individual, Justice Burton Roberts was also responsible, for at Sam's request during his trial, of making legal, Sam's name change to that of the alias which, Sam had chosen, Samuel Richard Carter. Hence, because of that, if one happened to have found themselves incarcerated in any of the myriads of the New York prisons and was looking for Sam Christian, they had a very difficult time unless, specifically told this, by Sam or any, of his associates in locating or, tracking him down during his stay, there.

As for Sam's trial, outside of going over the mundane and brief particulars of it, and the legal 'letters of the law', it was a pretty uneventful and un-exciting event with nothing exciting or major to write about unless of course, you were the defendant on trial there. Oddly enough, the most profound and deserving of being interesting thing that took place was, the cordial and almost amicable understanding and exchanges that took place during, and after the course of the trial between both Sam, and Justice Burton Roberts.

It was not that the judge, had forgot his charge, and he was not going to do it, to its fullest capacity. And it was not that Sam had forgot what he was up against, and was going to, let it roll over him, and come what may, either. Rather, what it was, was despite the existential and serious nature of what was before each that existed, the now un-seemingly, and almost unseen common and almost seemingly, lost nature of just being, human. And with that, at its conclusion, Justice Roberts did exactly what he had been charged to do, and Sam accepted his decision with the dignity and pride of, and as a man, was supposed to. That was true and despite, after he was sentenced, that he exercised fully, his right to seek further conciliation, and consideration to have lowered in the appellate courts, the sentence that the judge had rightfully, within the, or his boundaries of his charge and with compassion, had imposed upon him. To this, Sam did with no success as, the sentence that he received, was upheld there, in that regard, as well.

Upon sentencing him, Judge Roberts conveyed a few things to Sam, which had evinced to, the things just mentioned in regard to, the respect and civility that existed between the two. "A man with your intelligence shouldn't be in prison. Although I'm going to have to send you away for a little while, I have a feeling that you won't be there for long. I'm sure that while you're there, that you will be an example of that, 'a person can change'. To the prison authority, you won't have any problem from, or with, this man. And as he has requested, I want him treated like, and with the same fair treatment offered by rights as that, of the other prisoners. And also, as he has requested, I want him put in, General population. If you have any problems from any of the staff there Mr. Carter, I want you to contact me. In fact, it is my advice that, you all, should, study this man. Because if you do that, you will then find in him, a great deal about, and of, yourselves." With that, he then sentenced, Samuel, Richard, (Carter),Christian and later, as many of you all know now, Beyah to, three terms of 15 years to life, to be run concurrently. Concurrent meant that, Sam received one sentence of 15 years to life and that, he would have to serve 15 years before he would be, eligible for parole or that, he would be able to see, and walk the streets again. Sam then in turn, stated to Justice Burton Roberts, *"Your honor, I appreciate your giving me a fair trial."* and as he relayed to me, this was a statement that he, Sam truly, and sincerely meant. *"In fact, it is my advice is that you all should, study this man. Because if you do that, you will then find in him, a great deal about, and of yourselves." "In fact, it is my advice is that you all should, study this man. Because if you do that, you will then find in him, a great deal about, and of yourselves." "In fact, it is my advice is that you all should, study this man. Because if you do that, you will then find in him, a great deal about, and of yourselves."*

"Don't talk to me about no, ' yea, though I walk through the Valley in the Shadow of Death', I live, there! This statement, Sam was once overheard to have said to, I guess, a supposedly, and trying to change him well-meaning soul. If the term, 'The belly of the beast' had been designated to the whole overall prison system, then at the time of his sentencing, Sam had been committed to, the colon or rectum cavity of it. He had been committed to, Attica Correctional Facility. What had made this particular prison as I have stated, the

rectum cavity of the 'beast' was the timing in which, and he was committed there. As many may, and should recall is what has been termed, 'The world's most infamous prison riot'. As is mainly the cause at many prisons, this one, was the result of 'over-crowding', inhumane conditions and high tensions. In addition to those precipitants, the one that really, ignited the fuse on this particular one were, the same thing that, has caused problems since, the beginning of time, rumors. On September 8th, 1971 after a guard mistakenly took two prisoners away for punishment whom he thought, were fighting.

Word then quickly began, spreading around the facility that, they were being tortured. The next morning, after the whispers had turned to simmering then to, a boiling point, that was when, over 1000 prisoners commandeered a portion of the prison and took 42 staff members hostage.

Known for a large portion of its population being minority, the prisoners thought the warden to be racist, and that he, on a more than regular basis, had the guards under his charger inflict unspeakable brutality upon the prisoners there. They had wanted the federal government to first, come in and get an up-close and personal view of the things that they had suspected and were being subjected to, and then to, take control of the prison to improve its overall conditions to a more fair, and humane state. At the conclusion of the riot on September 13th, 1971, and at the behest of Governor Nelson D. Rockefeller, 39 people, 10 of them being, their own fellow prison guards shot by their own brethren, and the National Guard had lain dead.

Approximately two years later, by the time that Sam had been committed there, the harassment, abuse nor, the conditions had not changed very much if, at all. Justice Roberts had stated at the conclusion of Sam's trial that they, the prison system would not have any problems from Sam. He had also stated that, Sam would also, be an example. On one account, he had in a way, been partially wrong.

On the other account, he could not have been more, on the mark. However, this is not to state that, on the account that he had in a way, been wrong that, that was necessarily in, a bad or, negative sense either. That was because, with the likes, and assistance of such people as one, Jerome, Samuel, Rosenberg, Luis Manuel, Herbert Bliden and Marco R. Tedesco and a few others, that was exactly what, he had set out to do, being that example in a positive way that, Justice Roberts had stated at his sentencing, that he, would be. He wanted to cause problems for, not just Attica, but the prison systems as a whole. He, and they were hell-bent on, and just as fervently, as he had been when, he initially, joined up with the Nation of Islam on changing, and with some major successes, the way things were, or the normal acceptance of the way, that they were, in prison. In, Luis Manuel, Herbert Bliden and Marco Tedesco as well, but in Jerome Rosenberg especially, he could not have found or had, a better ally to have aligned himself with in, taking on such, a task.

They had set out, and wanted to bring about massive reform changes, conditions and conjugal visits such as those in places like, California's San Quentin Prison where, two weeks prior to the Attica riot prisoner George Jackson, the then love of one, Angela Davis was killed.

Jerome, or, 'Jerry the Jew' as he is more familiarly, and widely known, was also what, many considered to be, the 'Greatest', 'Jailhouse Lawyer' that had ever lived. Convicted in 1962, for the murder of two police detectives in a botched robbery while on parole after having, served four years at Comstock State Prison for a previous armed robbery, he had been incarcerated at Attica Correctional Facility ever since until, his death in 2009. After his family had sent him a set of law books before the days of, prison libraries, he had studied, and took a law correspondence course from the prestigious Blackstone School of Law. Never having had taken the bar exam (for evident reasons), he had helped hundreds of inmates regain their freedom, but was unable to get his own self, out of prison.

That does not negate the fact, that he had however, found a loophole in the system by the way of the gift from his family, and had managed (his greatest victory) to, have his death sentence which, he had initially received overturned and commuted to, a life sentence. It was he, that during the Attica uprising and riots first read, and then correctly surmised, as he ripped up the paper or agreement to demands that, "It wasn't worth the paper that it was written upon." The funny or odd thing worth mentioning about what Sam and those others, and what they had endeavored to do, that many, may have not taken note of was, the band of men that were enjoined together to accomplish that endeavor.

There it was, a black man, rather two, a Jew, an Italian and one of Latino, Mexican or Puerto Rican descent entwined together in a cause that, would benefit all of them, as a whole. In a world full of racial divide on so many minute and petty levels, I just feel as that is, or was, something worth mentioning. Afterwards, he had then been voted to the grievance committee there. To digress for a minute, something else worth mentioning was that, the first trailer visit at the Attica Correctional Facility following what they had accomplished was granted to, as you may have guessed, none other than, Sam himself. In regard to the grievance committee, this position was not one that was bought, or one where, other inmates were intimidated into, voting him into either. Because of his popularity in the prison, he had been voted to that position, 'fair and square'. And this is where, and how, Sam became a problem in particularly, for Attica Correctional Facility. Also, as it has been noted by many others on both sides of the fence that he, at the time of his stay there, had the largest visitor population or list that, Attica had ever seen. And, he had been visited by some very noteworthy people, his brother and old friend, the 'Champ' himself, Muhammad Ali being one, of them. All of this, he had done in a span of approximately, six months. After that, he was promptly kicked out of Attica. The reason for this was because, he had then by that time, done beyond imaginable comprehension exactly, what Justice Roberts said that he would do. He had become, as it had been stated for the reason for his expulsion, such a positive example and influence to, and on both, other inmates, convicts and staff members as well, all of whom, that he had called 'brothers' that, they felt as though, that positivity could possibly, become a threat, to the prison.

After a layover at Clinton Correctional Facility for approximately, another six months, he was then transferred to, Auburn Correctional Facility (The model prison for one of the things that he, 'Jerry the Jew' and the others, had set out to attain, conjugal visits) where he then, completed the majority of his sentence.

Now, the one thing that, one should keep in mind is that, during that time, not most, but all of the facilities or prisons in New York State were predominantly run by, as both Sam and myself jovially though he more seriously, the or, one of those, 'Good Ole' Boys' type prisons system or way. I don't really think I have to elaborate too much on, what that moniker or term, meant.

Friendship, being too strong of a word to use for fear, of its connotation being misconstrued, or taken in a wrong and negatively demeaning context so, while there, as I feel this more appropriate the word to use, he 'garnered' the respect and admiration of not only the superintendent at that time, whose name was, Captain Henderson, but many of the other guards and staff there, as well.

This feat, or achievement although in any other respect or regard elsewhere around that time, could have been viewed as nothing more than, mundane. There, it could and was viewed as, quite an accomplishment considering, as I have stated, the whole over-all environment and mindset of the people and the likes, that he, and the other prisoners there, had to endure. Once again, given all the things that have been said, attributed, alleged or even, and inclusive of the things that he has actually done outside of prison, in concert with the number of individuals that he had come across during his incarceration there, the former member of, 'The Family Four' (the church choir that consisted of him, his two sisters and his aunt) the former, Samuel Christian, 6X, Carter and now, Beyah a member then, of the Nation of Islam, had done good things and works on the prison system. That's how he spent his time while, doing time after, he had been sentenced to that time by, Justice Burton Roberts.

Out of the whole sum of time, that I had spent with Sam in putting together his story, although many of the things that I had written about him, that had taken place in his life or, the information that I had gathered and received about him while he was on the streets or even, after or before, he was sentenced to prison, had made some very profound and indelible impressions upon me, as our friendship grew, the most profound and most lasting things that he had or, would state to me that, would make an even more indelible and the most lasting impressions upon me, would come about during, and upon when, we were discussing his longest to my knowledge, that prison stint.

It was then, as he we were discussing these things that, I would get first, his insight and answers to the earlier questions that I had formulated in helping me to get an understanding of the myth, the legend and the man. It was also then, when I would get his own philosophies and perceptions on not, just what we, the public had formed about him, but also, on his deepest feelings on people, religion and the other aspects that make up the totality of a human being. Although again, as I had explained in the beginning on how, without inquiring of him, I knew that he had long ago, made peace with whatever may have perchance troubled his mind. It was also at this time, that I verbalized my inquisitiveness of wanting to really know that, if I was right in that presumption. "Brother Beyah, do you have any regrets for any of the things that had transpired in your life?" Not with a blink of his eyes, but instead, with a look on his face that seemed as if he knew eventually, as he was also waiting for, that I would get around to, asking that question, with unmistakable emphasis, unabashed or, unashamed certainty and with a sudden, firm and almost defiant as if daring contradiction lift of his chin he responded, *"No, not a thing!"* I then asked, "I mean, some people may attribute it to luck, but with all the things that you have been through," keeping in my mind, his staunch adherence or desire to follow as closely as he could, the tenants of the religion that he chose and practiced in his life, "I would have to attribute it to something more than that. When did you feel as though, you had been blessed or whatever one might call it, because again, given all that you have been through, one would have to attribute it to something more than just, proper planning?"

"Well, to finish the answer to your first question, regrets are for a person who, has not come to terms with his faith or God. And, to your second question there, when my lord favored me to find friends, amongst my enemies". He then went on to tell me the story of how he became and again, not wanting to have the connotation misconstrued so, if not exactly 'friends' then, on a more communicative, civil and amicable basis with one of the guards at Auburn that he called, and considered one of those, 'Good ole' boys'. *"I asked this guard one day, if I could borrow his ink pen. He looked at me, and said, 'Borrow my pen? I wouldn't let my wife borrow this pen!' So, I went and called my wife, and I had her to, send me a box of those gold-plated pens. And when they came in, I went to directly him, and gave him one and said, 'Here, I want you to have this, but do me one favor. If your wife asks to use it, let her use it please?' After that, he became one of my best friends. He used to come to me after that, and talk to me all the time. He used to say, 'Sam, you're different from a lot of the others here.' And he was one of the most racist guards there. After that, he started to change, and look at things a little different."* With a smile, I then asked him, "How'd you come up with or, what made you decide to do that? I mean, hell that was a lot to deal with, the racism and being in prison

and everything. I mean, considering who you were, and what they had known about you and despite what Judge Roberts said, weren't you worried that, they might have tried to do you some harm if, given the chance?" *"No, I was that way with all of the guards. Some of my best friends there, were Klansmen. And I prayed to Allah, to help me to make this one, and all those other men see. And he did. That's how I became who I was with, all the guards in prison and everybody else too."*

He then again re-iterated to me that saying, that he had become accustomed to saying the many times throughout our being together. This time however, as it seemed that, I had finally heard it in detail and for the very first time as again, he said it, in a way what seemed, as a sort of concession or way of absolution for not only, that particular guard's past actions, but the actions of others as well. *"No man is born a devil, it's a learned behavior."* I then asked him that, "Throughout it all, did you ever feel tired or, frustrated in any sort of way?" To this, he responded, *"I kept in my mind that, in addition to the fact that this is a trying world, 'If he tried the prophets or the others considered to be chosen then, why would I think that he would not try me, or you? Also, I kept constantly in my mind that, the progress outweighed the tiredness, and I used that, as encouragement to 'Hold fast to the rope,' and prayed through it, when it seemed, hopeless."*

'Water, seeks its own level.'

I guess, from the parts that I paid attention to in Science class when I was in High school, that in a sort of way, what he was describing, or alluding to in a sense though, with the descriptive applied mainly now, to human beings or, the character of human beings was called, the laws of 'Thermo-dynamics'. I had decided or rather, was compelled at this point, to revisit a couple of the initial inquiries that, and pardon me, I initially visited in the beginning of his story. As I had done a great deal of research in bringing together Sam's story, there was only one thing or point, that I had decided not to research until, at this particular juncture. And that was, the meaning or attribute of his name, Beyah.

But, before going into that, I want to share one more Sam Christian story that personally to me which, I think, it is the top of all the things that, up unto this point that I have heard, talked or even, written about. When, we had first began this project, he and I, Sam as expected, and is the natural order of life, had aged considerably since, all of his travails as, we all have and will. At that time, he was getting around with the use of every now and again, a walker. One day as, he and I were walking down a street, I stepped ahead of him a few paces because I wanted to know something and, I wanted to find out something, I wanted to find out if, I was just a writer to, him. We had been hashing over the book and we had been discussing people in general as well as, the many whom had travelled in, out and through his life. We had even discussed the ones that, had never even met him although, if you'd asked them, they would surely convince you that, they have. And it is for them mainly, that I have entitled his story as I have so. We were, at the point in talking about close associates when I shot my query out to him without looking back, but listening, praying and hoping in-tently. As, I heard the audible rubber and metallic bump as, the front legs of the walker made contact with the concrete signaling, that he had stopped abruptly with, emphasis and purpose. And what he responded with, brought a tear to my eye with gladness and joy although, I did not look back to reveal that to him. We were talk-ing about the sincerity of some brothers and how it seemed that, although they mayhap inside of their minds believe what they are saying, to him rather, it appears that they, are more friends than, the thing that they profess to be to him unless, it's something that they can benefit from him or, his name. In fact, as he stated verbatim, *"Some of these guys out here, say that they are brothers, but they're more like, good friends."* At that, I stated, "Like, you and me hunh?" That's when I heard, the audible metallic rubber meeting the concrete bump as he emphatically responded, *"No, you're my brother!"* Like Sam Christian wanted nothing more than, to be a soldier, I think one of the main joys or precipitants in my taking advantage of the opportunity that I had been given in addition to telling a good story was to, be nothing more than a good friend to, Sam Christian as I knew, from our time together, he's had and seen very few of them despite, what many may believe they are and have been to him. And as, I think we both achieved our initial wants and desires as sought in the beginning of this story so too, do I think we've both reaped that extra added reward of being able to say, that.

Once again, mind you again that, in bringing his story together, I had also, formulated a couple of delineations to get a vector or more insight of just who, this man was in the totality and scheme of it all as well as, the other things attributed to him. I was astounded at the sim- or rather, 'Sam-uel-arities' between the two as, I came to that point and time. "Now Brother Beyah," initially, myself included, people had or have the tendency pronounce his name or, attribute sounding like, 'Bay-ot'. Among them, a great number had or have the tendency, as he is quick to correct with the most defined enunciation and the sound coming out as, or sounding like, 'Bee-yah' seemed, to persist in pronouncing it in the former, of the two ways. This was another indicator of the 'many' that to him, who were not hearing, or listening. Although it sort of sounds like, ' Be ya,' or, 'be you' it means, 'One capable of, the ability to going to great heights and as equally, great depths.' Two things, which were spoken go lucidly through my mind given the time that, I had spent with him at this part of the delineations or, attribute here. The first were, the words that Judge Roberts had spoken upon sentencing Sam. "In fact, it is my advice that you all, should study this man. Because if you do that, you will then find in him, a lot about, and of yourselves."

Then, there were, Sam's own words, having been overheard to have been said to another at one time, *"Don't talk to me about no, 'yea, though I walk through the Valley in the Shadow of Death', I live, there!"* In going on, the attribute also states of Beyah's name that too, 'You are emotional and fixed in your opinions.' This certain delineations here, in describing the totality of the attribute, leads me to another assertion or conclusion which, in addition to being stressed previously, and verbally by others, was also, stressed verbally by Sam himself, and that was, in his belief of not only that, 'a person could change', but also too that, 'No baby could be born a devil' and that, it was a learned behavior.

The delineations further goes on, to describe of the attribute that, 'You are hospitable, sentimental,' Here, it is not only reiterated, but I am reminded of, or in his, and my mind of his, unadulterated will-ingness and openness in not only, letting me in and sharing with me first, his view or thoughts to be, on the totality of the, or his, spiri-tual and mental for observation and final preservation, the dissection and make-up of not only this particular, but also too, of all men and women, and his determination and again, willingness to give it as both concise, and fully exact as possible now once, and finally, for all.

The delineations again, further goes on to enlighten one of here sometimes, of the attribute that one could often appear, or seem or be considered, to be, psychic and sometimes, moody. At this, I am reminded of this one time when, we were in a car riding, him and me. A great number the feelings and things had been pluming through my mind, and transpiring around as a result of, my having decided to take on which at that time, I thought to be, a laborious but later becoming, a pleasurable ease and venture. It seemed almost, electrical in a very odd, and strange sort of way. We had been riding and I, having a feel-ing inside that, must have somehow, transcended so as being able, to be noted outwardly. I had looked over at him without a word, and he simply turned back to me with a smile and said as if seeming, to being able to have somehow picked up on my elatedness at this, and his remark was exactly how, I was feeling.

"I know. It feels so good that, it feels like you're going to die soon. You ain't ever had a feeling that felt so, good! I know. I know, how it feels. I've felt it before. That's God! He always, sends the help!" At this, after first smiling, we both literally, and outwardly then, laughed hard, and loud too. Because he knew, and described it to me, exactly, how I was feeling.

Now, on the side of 'moody', although there may be, the many others that, can conjure up, remember or envision, much more sobering instances of him on this particular part, in this delineation of his attribute, I however, can call to memory, one particular and more recent example of one instance, on a much more lighter in levity example of one, in regard to him to evince how, and much that, he could be so. I had went by to see him one day, to go over and discuss some of the things that we had went over the day before, and thus far, previously to that point. As I entered, I had taken note that, he had kept his eyes peeled to the T.V. save, to grant me every now and again, and as needed, cursory glance or response.

He had been watching, 'Hardwood Classics' on, one of those sports channels. And for, until finally after, all those hours that day when, I had finally given up on any hope of getting anything settled, from, or done with him in, or on anything that I would go into with him about, or in regard to his story as, he would only respond with something about one of the players or, of, and with something in regard to the game that he could, and would not, turn his attention from. And as we, are not talking about the younger, or a young man here, many may mistakenly in the mind, fancy a picture of a Sam Christian, going through the many transitions of say, Alzheimer's or Dementia. Take note however again that, nothing in that regard of the point we are discussing here, could be further, from the truth. That was because, as I had come to learn about Sam, 'if he chose, and decided that, he didn't want to, and wasn't going to move or respond in any condescending manner then, no one or anything, was going to make him do otherwise.' With that, and him in that regard, you could just either, love it, leave it, roll with it or, by it.

Here, the delineations of the attribute goes on once again further, to describe that, 'You are ruled by love and the lack of it, and feel the need to be encouraged and appreciated.' To evince to wanting that, and as to, wanting to be nothing, 'more than a soldier.' in that, to have it truly noted, and to the extent and willingness that one, and he, was willing to go to, and through to exemplify his understanding, meaning and desire to have acknowledged and reciprocated in both its most purest, form and term, love in its most grandest, of luster and connotation.

Next stated, in the delineations of the attribute with regard to 'Beyah', it is written, ' You have an eventful, exciting life.' Well, in that regard, if you know or had even heard an inkling of, the some of the things associated with, or of that, attributed to him, then you would also, come to the conclusion or surmise that, as many are in-clined to believe about him, that there, in that regard, not a truer statement, or example of understatement has ever been put down in any form or medium, 'spoken'. Next described of the attribute, ' You are versatile and have the ability to learn easily.' It is here, and where he, with his versatility and ability to have been able to, think and learn fast on his feet both, finally acknowledges verbally without any more 'beating around the bush' as he would often do whenever, I would broach upon him personally about his, and his alones feelings on not whether, but to the extent of racism and its effects that may have per-chance, affected him, in the deep and very profound way that it affects most of us, as I began again with my query of, and with, "Given, and after all that you have been through from, The Moors Science Temple to, The Black Panther Party to, The Nation of Islam and finally, to what you now, have come to known as, The True Religion of Islam, you mean, you're going to tell me, and still insist that, racism doesn't fully exist in this here country of ours, and has had none, not a one, really profound effect on any of the real motivators or motivations in regard to, or in conjunction with any of the things that you've experienced and went through in your life ?"

Finally conceding or more like, willingly relenting or maybe, just simple verbal acknowledgment as if, he had known all along, of its existence while yet, still viewing it as, something that he really didn't want to accept, realize or concede in regard to, it's unadulterated and 'good for no one's' reality really was, what it really was as he first softly, then with more rising conviction in his voice to, commiserates with me of his, knowledge in knowing, yet wanting otherwise, he then states to me that, *" Yeah, I knew that, in many of the things and transitions that I had went through, that it was at times, practiced against me. But, I was fortunate enough to, have always kept an open mind, and that has always led me to look, for the exception. And I always found it. That's because I also, always never forgot to ask Allah all the time to, 'Help me to, and make this man see."* Here, this thought has now become, trained in my mind to always think about what he means, when he says in regard to the people that he has encountered throughout his life in always, wanting to, 'help'. *"Still,"* and I believe him whole-heartedly, *"I never really had any color hang-ups although, I knew that racism existed, and it was, as I said, practiced against me, and I had seen it practiced against others."* And before he affirms with what, I have now ordained to be, as I have also chosen now, to call or, 'coin' it now, his trade-mark statement, he laces it up with another observation that I have heard he, and many others exclaim a time, or few. *"I never believed that, a person could not change. And that's what I've always strived to do was, help them change."* And after that, he followed again with,

"No baby, is born a devil. It's a learned behavior. If one can, learn something whether, good or bad then, one can unlearn it." as, it finally began sinking in of, the message that Sam had been seeking to have noted and relayed of, not just in regard to this book, but throughout and in regard to life, and the lessons that it had to offer, as well.

Learned Behaviors

Although, I had learned a vast amount about Sam from what, Sam himself, and others on and about, the various places that he had traversed, most precious of what I had learned or received from him, had come from when he was sharing with me on, his time spent while doing his time, for the sentence that Justice Roberts had imposed upon him. This was not only on, or with people like, Sonny, Frank, and the racist individuals or others that he had encountered. But also too, on if he could, anyone else as well, was his paramount observation of people and how, it was righteously advantageously best for one to use that observation to one's best advantage, that could and often times did, turnout to be, to the better and best benefit for all parties involved. And that was, in his observation of that in regard to, the rich and the poor and accountability. In that, was especially of how, 'the rich want to be honored.' So, to the betterment of the achiever was, having and keeping paramount the knowledge of helping him, 'the rich' on learning of how, to be so. In its simplest form, the job for the achiever was to, encourage he, that seeks to be honored and seen by such to others, to be seen by others in thereof, taking care of others. Others, in that regard being, the poor. Let us not forget that this philosophy, he had learned a long time ago from his mother which again was to, "Always take care of the poor and way-farer." In addition to that, this was also a concept that was re-iterated, and that he had never lost ever since, taking his Shahadda.

Taking the Shahadda is, the vows or covenant that one takes upon, his or her's taking an avowal of remaining committed to the folds and tenants of the Islamic religion. I had wanted at this point, to hammer home, or reverberate a point to as many as I could, the younger brothers and sisters on the streets so, I wanted and endeavored for him stay on, and expound upon somewhat, the note of prison and the end resultant of its futility for one that truly in their hearts, have the intentions of truly succeeding, or coming up from the adverse and often times, disparaging conditions placed upon most of them. "Brother Beyah, that being stated, can you give us your take on, 'Prison Pimping' or those that think of prison as something of a resort or, a place of resolve and escape from the hard struggles of life, in and on the streets?"

"In addressing that term, I will respond with one word in my description or rebuttal as such, of this," delineation or, *"term describing, one's choice, acceptance or choice of state of being as, anything of this nature being such to an extent, or something so enamoring and deserving of the title term, one word, and that word would be, 'ignorance'. In my offering, if my opinion is one of value to be seriously accepted then, of my most serious and ardent response would be that, anyone of that acceptance or belief should, 'Get rid of that life-style,' and thinking."* As, to a point of enlightenment or explanation on this part right here, Sam then said something that, many may have never thought, that they would have heard or, hear from the mouth of Samuel, Richard Carter nee, (Christian) now, Suleiman Beyah. He then relays that, he has at times, in and throughout his life felt, a small semblance of responsibility and precipitant for what had ultimately become, a wrong perception and that was in the, 'Don't Snitch' mentality that it became, not only a hindrance and detriment to progress, but also, an open-ended and ignorant freedom to the destruction, and violent end of the 'black' family unit, structure and or village, as a whole.

"Hold fast, to the rope!" *"However also, fall not, to the belief of that as, a point of contention in my life, of that assertion being*

incongruent to my feelings on, having regrets." said he, of whom the delineations also said, 'You are adventurous and willing to take risk to achieve your objectives' whom, was also overheard to have said that once again, *"Sometimes, you have to shock people to get them to think or, into, the action of thinking."*

It then, went on to define or explain in the description of the attribute that, 'In your seeking, of freedoms and opportunities to enjoy life, to make love, to go places and do things, unavoidable is that, 'one adventure must, and does, lead to another.' 'It was just the nature of the beast' so on described, the attribute in the search to find, 'new ways and new experiences' that, 'can't satisfy the restless nature' No one could dispute that observation, when it came to Sam. He did, even when and although he oft-times wasn't there, seemed to be, 'everywhere'.

'Honest and fair, because you know that this, is the only way to receive justice and honesty from other people.' One could, add in as a main precipitant in that regard as to, and why Sam had been able to do so, as described, in that most latter of that observation. *"The Help, will come!"* was, another one of those things that Sam was fond of saying, and most of the times, correctly. Now, although Sam had to ride alone physically, with his bid, it wasn't as if, he had went in there without any armor. As to his assertion of, 'wanting to be nothing more than, a soldier', he was serious and adamant in that assertion as in, if the ultimate endeavor of a cause seemed righteous and fair, then he, did not mind being led by those of whom or, what he commiserated with.

While along the time when, he and Donny had been rolling hard together, long and before, things had culminated to that then, present point that they were, he had been trying to get a grasp or, find the 'angle', with this certain individual. I mean, and man, was it plaguing his brain.

'Sometimes, you never know, the one, you may be looking for, may be looking for you'

The thing that, had been really eating at his mind though was, it was not as if either, he did not know this individual or, as if he were just someone that popped up in Sam's life while he, Sam was later along, on his journey of self-knowledge. Along with, *"The help will come"* and, *"One step prepares you, for the next step"* this adage, *"Sometimes, you never know, the one, you may be looking for, may be looking for you"* were some of the several, that Sam used frequently when he was elaborating on, or, describing progress.

As previously stated, the two, Sam and this other individual, had not only known about each other, but actually knew each other long before either's paths crossed at that later junction in Sam's life. In fact, their lives had been for lack of a better term, intertwined even as far back as, Sam's younger 22nd and South Street days. But, it wasn't until shortly before things had gotten to the extent that they had then when, everything began falling apart or began, to have been, being re-invented or re-structured when Sam began to realize how much, that he really didn't know this other individual. And when the thing that been eating at his mind about the individual finally began sinking in, it was then that, a relationship had been forged and bonded that has lasted long and well into even, this date. As again, I have stated earlier, there were a number of the gangs that roamed the streets of Philly back in the days when Sam, and his 22nd and South Street crew were roaming the streets that were, just as formidable or even rougher than he, and his crew were. And once again Philly or, the black ghettos being dissected the way that they were, many of these gangs were in more than relative proximity to one and another.

Again, in regards to South Philly alone, along the path of South Street itself, one could pass through several gang's 'turf', or territory. There, in addition to 22nd and South was first, 20th and Carpenter Street. After that, and in addition to, was Montrose Street, another gang that, as most of the other gangs in Philly used, took or borrowed the name of the actual street's name. Off to the right from there, and heading down into the part of the city that was mainly, inhabited by the Italians there was, 22nd and Tasker as well as, a few other crews. Then, after that was, **The Italian Market.**

Although again, the Italian Market was a hub of sorts, where practically, everyone from throughout the city did their shopping there for, the freshest of produce, meats and vegetables and such, and did not have a gang per' say, they did have the 'alleged', *'Mafia'* there, in that part of the city. Then after that, was a project or, a confine where again, that was inhabited by or, where more blacks were transplanted, placed or, inserted. And there, in a place at around 5th and South was where, while riding the 'blade' of dealing and co-existing on the most precarious of grounds with the Italians there nearby, was another one of the most, that were reputed to be, 'best' of the 'baddest' gangs in Philly called, home. This was the place, where that individual that, had been eating at Sam's mind prior to things going awry was from, 5th & South.

Not long, shortly upon, or there after the time, that he began eating at Sam's brain, he was known to, the Muslim community of the Nation of Islam simply as, 'Captain Clarence'. These days, as then though however, it was with, the greatest of reverence and true and honest respect that when his name was announced amongst the brothers and sisters of the community, 'Captain Clarence' that one, took note of the articulation and enunciation at which, it had rolled out of the utterer's mouth and expressions of devotion and sincerity as, they were pronouncing, and saying it.

This was the same man for whom, from which Sam, had abruptly awakened Donny at five o'clock in the morning from a deep slumber after a very trying and 'rough' night before to exclaim excitedly, **"I know what it is about that brother!"** That revelation, coming long on the heels of everything that had ever transpired between the two, all the way from first, the 5th and 22nd & South Street days through, their time together in the Nation of Islam and ultimately to both, their transitions to what is now referred to and accepted as, 'True Islam' which ascribes, prescribes and subscribes to being, a religion of peace.

And, as I am also now quite certain that, that revelation or affirmation may have also been assisted or bolstered in part as evinced in, Captain Clarence's earlier, as I had also stated earlier that, I would later expound on and reveal the 'who', in the handling of the situation with Jahbar or 'Nudie' as, he was more familiarly known at that time, and Dubrow's Furniture Store where, and when, he simply said, the two things to Jahbar or, 'Nudie'. Those two things, and Jahbar's response and actions thus afterwards yes, I think, were one of the main precipitants that played a large part in bringing that revelation brightly to light in Sam's mind when he again excitedly, and finally exclaimed to Donny late or, early that morning, ***"He's a religious man!"*** It was then, that he first simply asked Jahbar, "Did you do it?" And after Jahbar had confirmed to then, 'Captain Clarence' and later, and finally, Imam Shamshadin Ali (now, Brother Shamshadin as he has requested and prefers) that he had indeed done so, it was the thing that Shamshadin said or, next instructed that had solidified or, put the foundation under that revelation revealed to Donny early that morning on, and of, that day.

Shamshadin or 'Shams', as it was permissible and accepted by those, of the closest relationships in his intimate circle to address him as, then instructed to Jahbar, "Well, you have to give yourself over to those powers in judgment at this, that the question of recompense and justice, be served and met." With that, Jahbar did, as he was advised.

And so, was the adoration, faith and belief forged between Beyah and Shamshadin. It had assisted Sam in enduring the test that had been meted upon him, upon his serving, his time in, all three, the streets of South Philly, the First Resurrection and finally through, and to the, and their, final transition.

And so, the delineations went on to expound that, 'And, your personal growth is vital for you, and it is difficult to be tied down by rules and obligations.' For Sam, he, who wanted to be considered, but nothing more than a soldier, it was not that he had forgotten or had been forgotten as to in, what or who, he was along his journey and those, he had interacted with at points along, with it. Nor, had those interactions been in a souring or negative manner either. This was evinced in as when, the Minister, Louis Farrakhan came to Philly for 'Savior's Day', one year. It was then, when Minister Farrakhan with the wide eyes and bright smile at the recognition of an old friend, announced or proclaimed publicly in kind and in like, as he looked out amongst the audience and caught sight of Sam, "I don't forget where I come from!" With that, and arms wide, he then, beckoned Sam up to where he had been speaking from, at the Center on that day. There, with a kiss of brotherhood and remembrance he then, hugged Sam before the audience there in Philadelphia. That particular happening or event was approximately, two years before I, had been given this opportunity of writing his story.

It was Shamshadin both, in spirit and word that had served to Sam as, a beacon or, point of vector in spiritual guidance when he had first began to do his bid, and he, Sam had embarked upon the things he had encountered there during, his stay in prison, and the ways that he had developed, to navigate to his objective there, as well. Now, irrespective of any, and all of the other nefarious and 'not so shining' things that have been attributed to either, this was the relationship and what Shamshadin had become to, at and in, its most fundamental form in regard to, Sam or, Suleiman Beyah.

While extracting, working and walking with Sam, I would contend that it was there, that while doing nothing in-particular, was when I had gathered or had come to the assertion that both he, and I had reached the plateau or, endeavor that we both had initially, sought out to achieve. It was there, and here where, I had gotten from him, the answers to the questions that I had initially sought same to, in regard to him and his feelings, on these things. Those or these, were the vectors as, or if, you may recall.

As the attribute further stated, 'Your restless spirit might best be controlled by choosing the field of work that meet your demand for action and adventure.' Sam, had seemingly as of late, found, his calling as, a sort of travelling social worker as it seemed, in his liking of talking and conversing with practically, and almost every one and they likewise, practically, each and every one of those individuals that he encountered, as we would be walking along with I, learning and building with him along the way as, we'd do so.

I've not only saved, but added this last part here, for the cynics, the curious, inquisitive on-lookers and gawkers or those, just in search thirsting, for the dramatic or sensationalism. As to, 'The help will come', faith and belief in people, I asked, "Brother Beyah, when, as I know there must have been, people that turned their backs or felt a certain way, how did that make you feel if, at all?" To this, his response was that, he had held steadfast to the faith in the knowledge that God would reveal the truth to them at a later date when, they mayhap be more receptive to receiving it. This was the meat of the matter to me. This was the part that I had wanted to get off of, and of, Sam Christian.

These were the vectors that I had chosen. This to me, was where I was going to get to the essence in my mind of, the characters that made up conviction and firmness to it in, not just him, but all men being, humans, and humanity. On loyalty and dedication I asked him, "Brother Beyah, what went through your head when, you were shot that time that you told me about up in North Philly?" His first immediate thought as he explained to me, was for his man, Donny who had inquired of Sam who, was seemingly fading expeditiously after being hit, "Yo man, you're hit and you're not looking good! We got to get you and us, out of here! How we going to do this?" I then asked, "Brother Beyah, when did if at all, or, if you would permit it to be stated that, you felt like things were bigger than you, or that you were favored from a being higher, than yourself?" Deftly and expeditiously upon my completing that query he responded, *"When God, let me find friends amongst my enemies!"* To this, though as example, one could use as evidence his time spent in prison and the things that he, and those others had accomplished. They could also, use as example, the words uttered by Justice Roberts, "You should study this man," and, "You may find yourselves." But mainly, he was speaking of the whole slew of racism and people without conscience that he had encountered along his journey, and way. These to him, were the 'exceptions'.

I then asked the man who had been charged in approximately, just over, 40 crimes and seven of them being for murder, his feelings on those, that think as a first option, 'took pick up a gun', a wise one. *"They could never imagine the cost or, how deep, the decision of the act could cause everyone involved, and especially, for themselves."* "And again, to those, that think prison is acceptable?" *"They're foolish!"*

On life, "Brother Beyah, what is your perception or opinion on, life?" I'm sure like myself, giving all the things attributed to, and circulated about him, many desired the, or his, opinion on that certain point. Once again, as he had previously stated, and re-iterated as we were going along, *"Everything is designed to, send a message to your mind. Man, means, 'mind'. Woman, means, 'womb of the mind'. She gives birth, to thought."*

"Well, Brother Beyah, I guess it's a pretty good bet to say, I wouldn't be in error if, I were to say that we both know you were feared, but what are your feelings on, respect?" *"Respect, is a kin to love. You can't have one without, the other."* I am also quite certain that, from speaking with the many too that, for as great the number of people out here or there, that may have feared and despised him, there were also, a great and large mass populace out here or there, that feel or have felt just as strongly, in the opposite vector gearing towards, adoration in regard to, respect.

Of this next one, if I were somehow, summoned or were asked to give an opinion of which one of these, those being the vectors, that I find best as that, that somehow or in some way, summed up the essence of Sam Christian in regard to everything that had transpired with, and about him, I would have to rate this one as, very close if not, at the top of that hypothetical query or list of opinions asked. On loyalty, "Brother Beyah, define to me, if you would please, what loyalty means to you?" *"To be dedicated to a cause greater than one's self. The willingness to sacrifice to a cause other than, one's own."* I could expound on both, extensively and sometimes, spitefully jocular in saying how, this may have been evinced, in the many self-appeasing and self-aggrandizing stories and tales of lore of the many and their known, and remembered in some form or fashion only to themselves, of some personal interaction or dealing with him just for the sake of, making themselves seem bigger or somehow, more important than they truly were, or are. Or, I could, as I will, and was most certainly going to do anyway, keep it 100% concrete and factual and show how it was evinced, in his staunch dedication and loyalty to each of the plateaus along his whole tallied or, overall journey.

Did the man that wanted to be, 'nothing more than a soldier' feel betrayed or let down in any way sort for that loyalty? For one, *"No, because, I never had time to worry. And that was because, I was too busy praying for guidance which, always came."* Then, he added, *"Although yes, there may have been times where, I could have become angry like too, I could have become rich, but I've always decided to be, and stay true to the faith."* In his expounding here, I'm sure he was speaking in part on his, never having, to have been associated (in the terms of he, himself) with, (another misconception or error that was hung upon him whom, had spent over half of his life to the point of this writing, in prison) or, hung up on being a part of any of the things or organizations that he was attached, attributed to, or alleged to have been a part of, for the monetary or financial causes or aspects of it. *"In doing that, I found, what no amount of money or anger could ever achieve,"* again and, as I have stated about my initially noting upon, meeting and looking into his eyes, for the second time, and that was as he finished his statement, *"peace"*. Physiognomy; *'The art of judging a person's feelings by, their facial tics and movements'*. That was the Sam Christian that I had come to study, learn and had finally, from his own words, come to know about with, the tales and stories by, and of others, and, with physiognomics aside. In regard to my next query or vector on his feelings, or perceptions in regard with family or, the unit of such, would I be of the opinion that one, would be wrong in their assertion that given, prison and everything that Sam had gone or had chosen himself, to go through, that he too, in some large or major part, may have paled or could have been considered to have failed somewhat in that regard? However, also with, in regard to the pendulum swinging both ways, one, advocate or not, would have to consider that, or concede and not neglect in his dissertation or delineations of his feelings in regard to Sam that although, that stance could be considered a fair one in that, he had may have in many of the traditional ways, negated, paled or had failed in the analogous comparisons as described. But also, that one would have to, if not in the actual and physical respects remember then, like he had in, being mindful and remaining so, of the 'consciousness' of that respect as he had concluded, in his delineations or precept of same, in that regard. At this, despite any, and everything that had transpired in him being who and what he was, he did as well, and as best that he could, as he did, remain mindful or 'conscious' of that also, being, family. That, or they were mostly first, his off-spring as well as along the route, and the different communities that he became a part of. And like, many of the others outside of his actual off-springs or family, if in actuality, that he may not have happen to have been in the position at that particular time in doing so, they to whom, it may or may not have been happened upon at that particular time were, quite content if not all together happy in letting it be heralded or known as to the fact of their, relationship to Sam Christian which, was often-times, sufficient enough in accomplishing that task of covering that area or basis. And many, both actual and others, had as I have earlier, and throughout stated, did, and do utilize, and or abuse that privilege quite freely and without regard.

Again, as we had gone over previously, I then asked him again his feelings or precepts on 'Caring'. To which again, he re-iterated, *"It's an action word. You can't demonstrate or define it unless, you truly show it."* Although again, as one could consider this, a razor blade that once again, cut both ways in regard to Sam Christian and him being who, and what he was, one would also have to consider, the grand scale upon which Sam, and who, and what he was, had become during, and that time, also. And yet still, everyone *'ate'*.

I then switched gears or, vectors for a spell. "Brother Beyah, as people are sure to want to know, what was your reason for changing or making the transition from the Nation of Islam to the Sunnah religion of Islam? What was the cause or reason for you, to, making your decision of switching your belief from the Nation of Islam to that of, the religion and Sunnah of the Prophet Muhammad?" With Sam Christian deftness he then pounced upon, *"First, I began to question the teachings of, the Honorable Elijah Muhammad."* To this query, I then for the first time in our meetings and time together noted something that seemed minutely, to have pained or, had been bothersome to him in some small minute degree. Though still, as one mayhap, and may undoubtedly incorrectly surmise, this was not in the vain and crass sense that one, would expect. This was because, what seemed to have pained him was, to hopefully have not negated, misunderstood or neglected the fact, that his time spent with or, as being a member of the Nation of Islam as being one, in error or something, that could or should have been by-passed or avoided. It was to him, as he noted, a part of the transition or, natural order of things, that he had been so. It was, as in his growth, as he had come to know, the 'natural order of things' or, a thing that had been ordained. And he was not, as I had explained again most recently, as was evinced in, the reciprocation, ashamed of it. Because, at the time of the brief meeting with Minister Louis Farrakhan, he had been practicing the Sunnah religion for a large number of years.

In again, in addition to his adding as his reason for his decision in that, *"No baby is born a devil."* alluding to the fact that, it was a learned behavior or, 'Hate responding to the hate that, hate produced' also, he added that, *"I began to see that, it worked."* No doubt here, he was speaking in regard to, the precepts and other things that he had begun to learn as he became, more intrigued and learned of the religion.

It was also, around this same time that, he introduced Shamshadin to a few of the people very close to him that, as he was fond of saying as he truly meant it in many regards them, 'wanted to help'. Here, I am specifically speaking in regard to a few other people like say, a few more Sonny Viners, but in more genuine effects, and one, Warith Dean Muhammad (one son, of the Honorable Elijah Muhammad) who, was mainly responsible, for the transition amongst a good number of the members in the Nation of Islam in the direction of 'True Islam' as it had finally began, being manifested on a large and expeditiously scale throughout America then.

Although even now, as I can't speak in regard to the rest of the country although, I'm quite certain that a vast portion of it has an awareness of him, but one thing I can state with certainty in regard to Sam and both the cities of Detroit and Philadelphia as this, has been affirmed by a number of important people in his life from that area, it was because of Sam and who he was, or rather, the things that had transpired about him that it, had spread as quickly it did, in the both of those two cities.

Sam during our conversations had once told me, he had asked

his mother why it was that, she had talked to herself on occasion. He then said, his mother's response was that, she liked talking to intelligent people. In the direction or way, that he had decided to go in making his transition to true Islam or the Sunnah of the Prophet Muhammad (P.B.U.H), he had found the best of intelligent help and assistance to, not only converse with, but also, to help him along the way on that journey as well, in the likes of both, Warith Dean and Shamshadin Ali as well as, a number of a few other prominent people that had been, and come into his life. On devotion. I then asked him his feelings on, that precept or concept. Again, although many may view his response to this query with raised eyebrows, they would also have to admit on a larger scale that, in regard to Sam and again, the things that he had done and or, was associated with that, one would also be, hard-pressed to find a more on point, or exact delineation to define a person as, such. *"It is a sensitivity and concern for another or other's health and welfare and not, just in the physical sense. It is a blessing in the lesson of, 'Humanness'. It is the thing that keeps one human. On its deepest level, it is a question and answer with God."* Again, at this, I was reminded of the conversation that he stated that he had with his mother in regard to talking to herself and her response, "I like talking, to intelligent people". One would have to agree that, you couldn't find a more intelligent person or being than that, to talk to. I then asked him about his feelings or concept on, 'Gratitude'. *"To me, gratitude is, being grateful and appreciative to God. That is the highest form of gratitude. When you help another to see it, you help them to realize that, 'although you can see with your physical eyes, you can't see the spiritual unless, you're connected to it."* In that, as the analogy was made earlier in regard to, the differences between how people of color and non-color worship God, one could, or would have to concede then, that Sam, in his professing of wanting to be 'nothing more than a soldier', in that all he had went through from first, his Christian upbringing to and through his, or the point of and when, we first began on this story was truly and in fact, and had always remained so, very spiritually connected.

Thinking about the next, I was then reminded again, of one of the things that one of the brothers had said to me, in regard to Sam. "On humility?" Before he began with, *"Asking God to humble one's self,"* and adding, *"I asked him, to not let me become arrogant or 'Big-headed"*, I had thought back, "If there were ten people in a room, you couldn't tell which one, was Sam. That's how quiet, and humble he was. He wasn't all boisterous and loud or any of that stuff." Then he concluded, *"These are the things that, 'blinds' one."* speaking on the point of, the ills of being, 'arrogant' or 'big-headed'. "Brother Beyah, on Determination?" I then, asked. Using probably, one of the oldest adages ever used that always, sounds appropriately befitting and modern to seemingly each, and mostly every situation he then responds, *"Plan your work, then, work your plan!"* I have to admit that, although I had heard that adage a many of times, it had sounded kind of, extra cool hearing it from Sam and especially, in the cool and sort of natural off-handed and matter-of-factly way that he had shot it, right back at me. Then finally, before I had gotten to the last and most important of all the vectors and reasoning for, and on this writing in addition to, 'clearing the air', the most prominent and most emphatic vector, direction or reasoning in my approaching his, or this story from the direction and manner in which, that I have chosen to pursue it so, "Conviction. What, if any Brother Beyah, would you give the public and or, the inquisitive in regard to conviction and your precept or perception of it?" Again, given all now, that you know about Sam Christian what would you do, if given the same set of circumstances, opportunities or situations? Honestly now, while I expound on his response, you can take this time to dissect in your mind of, what would be the outcome? Would things be the same for one, as they were, or turned out for him? Your quiet, introversive and solitary 'moment-of-truth'. And for the second or third time as, I have expounded on, for and as many times, he then responds, *"Serve God as though you see him and know that, if you don't see him, he surely for certain, sees you. You got to have faith in him first, and especially. Then, you have to have faith in all his servants, messengers and his prophets. If you get lost from that, then you are truly lost like, and worse than, a blind man stumbling about in darkness."* For this man who again, only wanted to be, 'nothing more than a soldier', it was evident for anyone who knew, knew of, or about Sam and or, some of the things that had gone on about, behind, because of, and over him, that indeed, he stood strong and steadfast for, and in his convictions.

I then finally, asked him about that one last little thing. That thing in which, at the very end of every story, it does or does not evince of the characters that very fine and oft-times, delicate position or trait called, 're-deeming' quali- or 'ties'. That capability or connection where one is defined again, in the most rawest or defining essence as, or of being, 'human'. "Brother Beyah, and finally, can you leave us with your definition of, 'Love' and of course, your perception or precept of it?" First, he gave me as his definition, *"Another action word that, cannot be expressed without action. It grows as, you grow."* He then, affixed to me, that stare. That one where, while and when, and throughout as we had been building, bonding, teaching, learning, writing and rapping he would affix it as, and when it seemed, a question that was asked by myself was either, one that I should have been able, or it, should have damn well, been able to have been be deduced, surmised or one, should have, or had the ability to have already known the answer to. Or, it was otherwise two, one that I, specifically, should not have asked out of knowing, the foolishness of even asking so ludicrous, a question. In any case, after all that he had shared with me, you, I or, all of us, it was, or should have been quite evidentiary of his commitment to that end, in love that he did, go through, and in addition to, a lot of the ways, that he went through them that, that question need not to be addressed when it came to him, and there, in that regard concerning love, in its rawest and most devout and meaningful connotations of the term. And, on that, we had concluded.

Now, for you, the reader, that was not the conclusion for Sam, but his story.

To evince my point as I have earlier stated in and that, not many, and as well as, Sam included, on the more conventional and normal crass and vane sense, was left without scars as a result of those times, and the things that had transpired during, and after, as a result of them. Even, if one wants to go so far as to, want to put, or lay blame to Karma or something of that degree for them happening. As his very soon to be parole officer by the name of, Kabba had advocated for him that, "This man does not need to be in prison. He needs to be restored to society, to show people how to stay out." It was time for Justice Burton Roberts observation ("If they study him, they would see themselves") to be realized. Upon his release and parole in November of 1988, it was then for a spell, that things or, as it may have seemed that Karma, in some sort of way or how, had then been visited upon him also. As for that short minute, he had then 'tripped' a little, and hit a slight bump in the road along his journey. When he was released, there was a pretty big party of sorts given in his honor. Although, I did not give much thought or consideration to the location then as, it was being relayed to me, it was in either, as I believe that it was told to me, Las Vegas or Atlantic City. It was well dressed and adorned with all the right or 'wrong' things. There was the money there. No, there was nothing so as big as, brief or suitcases of money there being given. But there were, large envelopes handled and handed. Then, there were the women or, the, 'good-time' girls ready, very willing and waiting there, as well. There were a number of 'good brothers' there, also.

Mixed in with them too, were a great number of the reptilian and false smiling ones, as well. Sprinkled strongly about too, and in like amount, with the massive amount of cocaine and other inebriants that wafted through later were, a great number of not-to-be-kept, false and in-sincere promises and negotiations goings on.

Then, topping everything off there was more drugs. And finally, as fate, luck or, as it had been hinted at, plan would have it, the end came. In mostly, the literal sense rather, the end of the party, or the weekend had come to a conclusion. At that conclusion, after all the ones that had truly cared about Sam's 'life' had exited and those, who had truly 'respected' him had done likewise then, there were those, that were also truly 'loyal' that had followed suit and exited. In that exodus amongst them too, were also those, that he had considered, and rightfully so, as they really were to him, 'family' and those that truly, truly and really cared about and were, devoted in the strongest sense of the term to, and that loved him that had left also. All, that were in attendance at the gathering however, before they had parted ways with him at the affair, had expressed their gratitude and avowed their loyalty. That was even true of, those that were also in attendance that probably, meant him no real good will or fortune. For this kind, and or, kind-like showing or expression Sam too then, expressed his being humbled, by the kind, and or, kind-like gestures or showing of appreciation for him. After all that happened, then Karma or, 'the damndest thing', had taken place.

It was then, and there, for a short brief period that, the man who had inherited as a trait from his mother by nurture and example of not drinking as he had, "never seen her drink anything stronger than a soda" and who had never even, smoked a cigarette because as he stated to me, *"it almost choked the hell out of me"* and had never done a drug in his life, had become, or was, for the first time in his life, addicted and under the spell of one of those intoxicants in the form of, cocaine. Then, after a brief period of approximately a year and a half after that, or his last hit of cocaine and the last professional 'good-time' girl had left him alone by himself in that hotel room that wee-early hour of that fateful morning, Sam had stumbled around and about, in the places that he had once traversed through and about in earlier years solidly, in the insidious grip of the apothecaries that he had fought so hard against, and to prevent.

After that, and then, with the much focused determination and help of those that, as I most had recently stated, that truly, truly loved and cared for him, and they were, and still are many, Sam once again found, or regained his 'conviction', reason and determination and kicked his habit.

It was then after that, approximately, seven to eight years later when, I had met him again for the second time in my life, and was bestowed with this opportunity to chronicle not, the well circulated stories that all may have read or heard in regard to the *'Black Mafia'*, but his, Samuel Richard Christian now, Sulieman Beyah's life.

Before we had concluded, I had asked him one more, to me, very important question. His response was, *"No, it was never a black and white issue. It was about trying to uplift a people both, black and white who were still, in a state of ignorance, deceitfulness and treachery."* At this, I will conclude that, in the totality of everything and all that I have written about, and that had transpired as well as, that which I have heard, I am reminded of a statement that I had heard from many of the brothers that were really in the first resurrection as well as, Sam included, and a part of what had transpired in Philadelphia. *"We were not bad people. We were sincere people, whose sincerity was abused."*

In conclusion for you the reader, it is also my contention that whether, advocate or opposition, there will always be one of the viewpoint or 'beast' to have, that hunger, lust or validation of that stance fulfilled, quenched or deemed righteous. In regard to the *'Don't Snitch'* mentality or, 'mis', pre- or conception that has been so highly, touted and laid upon Sam and those, of his associates. In addressing or, laying that blame on Sam or, the alleged, *'Black Mafia'*, in addition to that concept being something that, was in existence a long time before 1939 and again, the *'Black Mafia'*, in the beginning, that was not the concept. For these men initially, when a number of the things or murders that took place, it was mainly about, cause. Again, with these men initially, it was not so much the matter about, or of, outside perceptions and how the outside public felt about it. But rather, what it was in its delineation and raw fundamental form, was a matter of *'what had to be done'*. That was just the nature of that business or again, that beast albeit though, for either, 'religious' or more, homogeneous reasons whose hungers, lusts and or, validations had once again, been sought, or had to be met. Such primal deeds and especially, as well, as those initially so for cause, did not require the benefits and luxury of speech. What had to be done, had to be done. What was done, was done.

And after it was done, the hard and cold reality in that, was that, 'no amount of frustration over wishing or hoping, could change what was done or could bring back, what would, and could be no more.'

Again, that was before, what became, ignorant self-hating novelty and normal without feeling, sport. At least wise so, that's how it began there, anyway.

Then finally, in regard to the name, title or delineation of Suleiman, that's exactly, what it is! A title, and its meaning of Turkish descent translated being that, 'a title of respect' or, 'man of peace' or rank.

And despite whatever one may think of Samuel, Richard, Carter, Suleiman Beyah, Christian, there are many more that are of, or hold the opinion that, in his character and convictions were ensconced all of those, and the other attributes.

In regard to the man himself, as I last checked when were together during the month of his birthday which, we both share, he was fine. But this was something that I knew, a long time before that, as I have stated about when, we first embarked upon this project of presenting to you the reader, his story.

But, it was outside of the masjid that day which I also, spoke about earlier, when I myself, in my own heart knew, that he was, and would be fine.

That was the day when Donny, and myself had that little misunderstanding. As we sat there, with our backs turned to each other with him, Sam and I and he, while facing towards the east and I, towards the west. As we sat there with our backs barely touching and him, never even turning to make eye contact or taking a break from seemingly finally, being able to enjoy and take in fully, God's true gifts being, the simple light breeze and the sun's luminance that was letting him reflect and take in the blessings that had been bestowed upon him throughout his life and its journey and he, looking and feeling as though, I was sitting there with my own father and he said to me, what I had stated earlier, that he said in regard to Donny about, *"Don't worry about Donny. I even, put him on my 'pay him no mind list' sometimes."*

And then, and still, without looking at me, as I felt in the warmth of our backs touching, the love, kinship and true brotherhood when he said to me, *"All these guys are waiting for Superman to come back and he's not coming back."*, I knew, he was, and would be fine.

Malcom X once said in an interview that, *"Those who know, don't tell. Those who tell, don't know."*

In regard to Sam Christian, and by his word, permission and faith, I have told what I know, and know, what I have told, to be the truth.